TO A FELLOW ISLAND PARKER.

SIMPLER TIMES

A MEMOIR

Dale A Swanson

ENJOY THE READ!

5-22-2024

D1712956

SIMPLER TIMES

A MEMOIR

D. A. Swanson

𝓡𝓟𝓡

Rainy River Press
6106 Birch Road
Prior Lake MN 55372

Simpler Times

Print ISBN: 978-0-9863267-6-9
E-book ISBN: 978-0-9863267-7-6

First Edition: December 2019

Printed in the Unites States of America

Published by
Rainy River Press
6106 Birch Road
Prior Lake, MN 55372

www.dale-swanson.com

Acknowledgements

The Triune God gave me the most awesome parents from which to begin building a life of promise. I cannot imagine a better childhood in a more perfect environment than that which they gave me. The Village of Island Park, with its 500-plus acres of convoluted gravel roads winding through hilly woodlands, and around swamps, offered untold riches to a young boy.

I also wish to thank my high school classmate, friend, fellow Island Park resident, and grammar perfectionist, Sally Liu Lane, for her grammar expertise.

Last, but not least, thanks to my wife, Diane, who has given me the supreme gift—the most beautiful family one could ever wish for, and the real reason I live a life of joy.

These short stories are memories of my family and life in the 1950s.

This Book is Dedicated to:

*Jon Storke—My friend from the early years,
a highway accident took him way too soon.*

*George Farnham—voted as most talented by his high school
classmates, he died on the Island at Avalon Park.*

Other Books by D.A. Swanson

"My story is about anticipation, uncovering what lay ahead, and the reckless abandon of youth as we pursued each day—in the moment."
Dale A. Swanson

October in Minnesota can be fickle. In 1949, it was warm and not yet ready to yield to the first hard freeze. My birthday was renowned for beautiful weather. This one marked my seventh year and would stick in my mind for the rest of my life. The party has long been forgotten; the gift, the giver, and the place, however, remain.

We stood on the flagstones laid in freshly worked earth not yet seeded but destined to become a sea of green that will meet the stone edges. Five of us squirmed and fiddled as my father hunkered where the walk met the road and prepared for the launch. A gaggle of boys doing what boys do best, poking and prodding, dodging this way and that to avoid the retaliatory strike.

"You boys ready? Here we go."

Dad rose from his crouched position and took a few hurried steps. Amid a hiss and muted scream, the rocket jetted upward. Up, up it went into the azure autumn sky. At the very pinnacle, when it remained stationary for what seemed like minutes, the miracle happened. A small parachute popped out of the nose, filled with air, and the rocket drifted down.

As much as the ascension impressed, my mind sees the blue sky behind the gift, the blue that ended abruptly when cut off by the crimson and gold adorning the October trees opposite the road.

It drifted; swinging on tethering strings from the cloud above, and disappeared behind the hedge marking our property. With a gleeful 'yip,' amid much shouting and confusion, we charged, each of us intent on being the first to the prize.

Contents

Prologue

The Village of Island Park
Lake Minnetonka, Hennepin County, Minnesota

The island, roughly five hundred acres, was heavily treed mostly with maple, ash, oak, and elm covering the rolling topography, and it was pocked with swampy low areas where huge cottonwoods stood as sentinels and the sweet smell of the peat bogs soothed the senses. At the turn of the century, it was a summer retreat for the well to do, with a culture boasting afternoon cocktails and organized tennis matches between the handful of settlements with names like Wychwood, Pembroke, Arden, Avalon, and Chester.

As more people became year round residents the horse was replaced by motor vehicles and footpaths became a hodgepodge of twisting, turning gravel with dust billowing from the underside of Detroit's contributions to progress. Like a plate of spaghetti, these roads were capable of confusing the most scholarly visitor, and provided us with endless opportunities to misdirect the unwary until we imagined them nearly dying of thirst, unable to exit the labyrinth.

By 1947 refrigerators were replacing the icebox, most telephones were on a party line, hitchhiking was the method for distances too great for the bicycle, and kids didn't sass their elders without fear of retribution.

The war had ended, and the men returned to replace the women who had supported the effort by working assembly lines in their absence. The age of the Baby Boomers was upon the land and many Moms stayed at home spending their days raising us, managing the house, and maintaining and enhancing the local social structure. The times ensured strong bonds between neighbors. The result was a shared responsibility for every kid on the island, which allowed us to roam the gravel roads and woods without a care in the world, playing from morning till night, our parents secure in the knowledge that *someone* knew where we were and had their eye on us.

And God had a presence in our lives. How else could we have survived our own innocence and the foolish things we did? There were no mandatory seat belt laws. Heck, it was an adventure when we went anywhere in Dad's car. We rode our bikes with reckless abandon, never a thought of wearing a helmet. We climbed to the very tops of trees and tempted death a thousand ways. We swam the channels, bridge jumping as close to passing boats as we dared. We built fires with matches pilfered from our parents and we experimented with cigarettes and smoked weeds from the swamp. We stole watermelons and apples. We tipped outhouses. Like our contemporaries, we pooped in a bag, placed it on someone's doorstep and lit it on fire hoping they would stomp it out when they answered our knock. We explored language, particularly words that were never used in our own homes, which led to a swearers club that lasted for a few hours at most.

Why did my family settle here?

In 1945 it was considered remote, five minutes from nowhere by the rational people living in Minneapolis; they considered it a one hour drive to mosquitoes, bad roads, and living conditions better forgotten.

The answer to "why" would reside in the future—with a grandfather I barely knew.

CHAPTER 1

My Swedish Roots

I was sixty-seven before I learned that Grandpa Swanson wasn't an only child.

It came unannounced and unforeseen, a letter from Sweden that would expand my world beyond my imagining, an introduction to a family, my family, that I never knew existed. The writer began with a brief introduction then went to the heart of the matter: *Was my father's name Allan O. Swanson? Born...? Died...? Was my grandfather's name Johan O.K. Svensson? Born...? Died...? If that is the case, we are cousins.*

"Huh?"

Your grandfather had nine brothers and sisters.

"Huh?"

I composed a carefully worded email and sent it to the address included in his letter that I was certain was a ruse.

His reply arrived by email the next day, and it was like someone poked me in the temple with a fork. It included the names, birth, and death dates of ten siblings, the second oldest in the family being my grandfather. To seal the deal, he included a copy of the very picture that hangs on the wall in my office. In it are my grandfather, grandmother, father, and uncle—until the arrival of the letter, the extent of my very small family.

How in the world could this be true? Mom and Dad never talked about the family's background, but to keep something like Grandpa's nine brothers and sisters to themselves seemed almost criminal. Neither of my sisters was aware of family beyond our small group. Perhaps our parents were never told? Many of my Scandinavian friends tell me that their parents never talked about ancestral ties. We heard nothing of aunts and uncles unless they lived close by, and even then, there was never a glimpse into family history. Why were my grandfather's siblings pushed aside, lost forever to family not yet born? It was as though my past and that of my family had been hijacked. Why? Was there something being hidden, some nefarious deed associated with the family? Was some dark secret from the past being concealed?

The answer would lie with my newfound second cousin in Fårbo, Sweden. His name is Bosse Hjalteryd, and his grandfather was Grandpa Swanson's brother. Bosse has been studying the family ancestry for the past 25-years. Of necessity, his methods were old-school: church records, Parish land records, courthouse documents, and hardcopy archives wherever they could be found. I was to learn that within our family were Dukes and Counts, Kings and Queens, actors, and farmers, and merchants, rich—poor, and everything in between.

It seems there was nothing to hide, no criminal past, nothing begging concealment. I think the reason for neglecting family history boils down to two possibilities. The first deals with Scandinavian stoicism, which includes the inherent desire for privacy and understatement of facts. Few that know the inner working of the Scandinavian mind will argue that point. The second, and I believe it to be closer to the truth, is the mindset that developed as a type of self-preservation after leaving everything they knew and loved behind when they immigrated to their new country. Many were in their teens, and even more, were in their early twenties like my grandpa. How difficult it must have been.

It would be left for me to explore Grandpa Swanson's life and uncover details before they are lost forever.

* * *

The search started in my study, where he stands erect and proud. A handsome man, ramrod straight in his uniform, saber hilt visible at his left hip, left arm hanging comfortably at his side, hand protruding from the festooned sleeve of the uniform jacket. He stands facing us, right forearm resting comfortably on a studio prop of a broken tree. He seems to be missing a good portion of the index finger on his right hand. Square jawed and magnificent in the uniform of the Swedish Ranger Company 35, in which he served for five years. This is my grandfather, Johan Oskar Constan Svensson, as he was in the old country.

Grandpa John Oscar Constan Swanson

Hanging to the left of his picture is his U. S. Naturalization Certificate dated March 10, 1944. Personal description: age-67, sex-male, color-white, complexion-fair, eyes-blue, hair color-gray, height-5 feet 8 inches, weight-179 pounds, visible descriptive marks-right hand fourth finger amputated.

Born on May 2, 1876, in Kristdala, Sweden, he arrived in America May 6, 1903.

He is the reason we moved to the island.

* * *

Grandpa and Grandma Swanson were married on April 14, 1909, in Anoka, Minnesota, and they located to a farm in St. Francis. Grandpa Swanson was a farmer with all the skills necessary to be successful.

I have two clear memories of Grandpa.

The first finds me in the front yard of the island home with the family. The south-facing house sat about sixty feet from the narrow gravel road that crested the hill upon which the house sat. I was three years old, and Grandpa was holding me. The charred ceiling boards in the largest screen porch I'd ever seen fascinated me as I wondered about the fire that had caused them.

The second, and most vivid, is of Grandpa cresting the hill from the hollow just west of the house, scythe over his left shoulder, cotton shirt visible beneath bib-overalls, brimmed hat pulled to his ears.

I have the feeling that he wasn't a very happy person, and had I been older, I would have likely been afraid of him. His countenance was serious, and in many photos, he looks stern and unyielding. Therein lies the dichotomy. It seems impossible that a man described in such a manner could raise a son as in love with life, as outgoing, respectful, responsible, and as downright likable as my father. I asked my older sister, Jill, what she remembered about Grandpa. Her reply, "He was another Daddy."

In a series of pictures of Grandpa as a young man as well as those taken before the move to Minneapolis, he looks happy, almost cavalier in some. Only in the later years of his life does he appear to have changed. A severe injury to my grandma seems to have placed him on a downhill slope that prevailed until his death.

Grandma Tillie Sander/Swanson

According to Jill, the injury occurred when Grandma fell from the haymow while putting up hay. My Rapid City Aunt, Margaret, writes that my grandmother was injured during a vicious storm. She was caught in the field, and while running for the barn was hit with windblown debris. Whichever is true; she received a back injury that affected her mobility for the rest of her life. They left the farm and moved into a small house at 3458 Newton Ave. N., Minneapolis, in the early 1920s.

With a farmer's aptitude for things mechanical, Grandpa found employment at Waterman and Waterbury, a hot air furnace manufacturing company in Minneapolis where he was a member of the United Electrical Radio and Machine Workers of America, local 1140.

He paid the mortgage on the Newton house in full on April 21, 1938. The good feeling that must have accompanied outright ownership of the house was short-lived. In 1939, my Aunt Margaret was pregnant with their third child when uncle Stanley, Dad's younger brother, began falling behind and unable to keep up with him when the two went pheasant and duck hunting. Stan became weaker and weaker while suffering through test after test until he required hospitalization, finally passing away on the seventh of June, 1940, of complications caused by testicular cancer. Margaret delivered another daughter, Bonnie, seven days later, to join Susan and Gwendolyn as the third of Stanley's girls.

Grandma was devastated, and Grandpa must have felt a deep sorrow for as long as they remained in that house. The Newton Avenue house stands today virtually unchanged from when they lived there in the 1940s. They finally moved to the island in the spring of 1945. He bought lots 8 through 22, Block 7, Wychwood Edition (now 4650 Manchester Road).

Grandpa must have longed for the farm where familiar sounds and smells could permeate his senses, where he could sit on an open porch in the evening and hear the frogs and crickets in their symphony of night songs. Where a man could burn his autumn leaves as naked branches jutted boney fingers, pointing to the future in anticipation of the icy winds of winter.

I can imagine the feeling that ran through him when he traveled to the island. How much it must have reminded him of his native Sweden. Back home, with the scarcity of land, he would never have been able to buy what he could in America. It was wild. It was sparsely populated.

He likely viewed it as his own little piece of heaven. Here was a place where he could improve the land: clear brush, cut timber, dynamite the stumps, tend the apple trees, and transform the hollow adjacent to the house into a space of beauty.

Dad and Grandpa worked on the house after Dad's day job at Strutwear Knitting Company in Minneapolis.

* * *

Island House

The island house, built at the turn of the century near the top of the hill, was designed as a summer retreat with a screen porch facing south and running the full width and halfway along each side. It had a screen door in the middle.

The west wing of the porch became the summer dining room and was accessed by French doors leading inside. The food always seemed to taste better when accompanied by a soft breeze and the earthy smell that hung in the air after a summer rain.

Mom and Dad moved us there in the summer of 1945. The first priority was to make the old place livable for our family, namely four adults and two children. To that end, Grandpa hired a carpenter with ties to the old country, name of Swanson. Although, no relation to us, he was the framing carpenter who, much to Mom's displeasure, became the finish carpenter for all the improvements that would be made.

The changes were made while we were living there, and it nearly drove Mom to an early grave. She had her own ideas of what she wanted, but Swanson pretty much ignored her requests, preferring to do things his way. His stock answer was simply, "Vell it's flenty good nuf fer ne-body." My sister, Jill, remembers that Mom cried a lot during this period, and the stress triggered her asthma, actually landing her in the hospital on numerous occasions. It got so bad at one point that they thought she might die.

Dad brought me to see her. The first thing I noticed entering the hospital room was the heat. It was the first time I'd visited anyone in the hospital, and I expected to see doctors and nurses hovering over a well-lit hospital bed. What I saw scared the daylights out of me. Heavy curtains covered the windows and only a single floor lamp lit the small room. Midway between the door and the covered windows, the bed was tucked against the wall. The mood was somber, and as I approached at my father's side, my stomach tightened, and my breath caught in my throat as I saw my mother, head elevated, a plastic oxygen tent over the top half of her body, her breathing labored. I stood mute the whole time, not knowing what a person does in that situation. Finally, we left the room, and there was no doubt in my mind, no matter how I died, it would not be in one of those hot, dark rooms.

Back then, the prescribed home treatment for asthma relief was a product called Asthmador. It was a powder that came in a green tin with an oval, pry-off, recessed cover. The powder was scooped from the tin with the cover, filling the recess, and then lit with a match. It would spit and pop without flaming, and the resulting smoke was inhaled to open the airway. Poor Mom…she spent a lot of time hunched over her Asthmador.

Swanson, the carpenter, had a habit that drove Mom to distraction. The inside walls were plaster and lath. Swanson chewed tobacco. When you have a mouth full of tobacco juice, trowel in one hand, mixed plaster trough in the other, and you know you can't spit on the floor, what do you do? Well, you spit in the plaster and trowel it onto the wall. Asthmador, here I come.

That first summer, we got our water from a community well at Avalon, a park on the shores of Lake Minnetonka. Dad filled a large metal milk can, and it was ladled out to drink, or heated on the stove for washing dishes. Most times, we bathed in the lake, which Dad seemed to enjoy.

The summer homes on the island had no wells, hence no need for plumbing, so the ubiquitous outhouse was found in close proximity to the main house. Ours was attached to the horse shed behind the house.

* * *

Forward thinkers were abundant in the early island years. One of our neighbors, in anticipation of running water, put in a kitchen sink with the drain merely running through a hole in the wall. Strictly temporary, nonetheless, providing the most succulent tomatoes you ever tasted, self-planted from seeds washed down the drain, they were ensured of enough water to grow to mammoth proportions.

Our house was seeing improvements. The bedroom on the east side was divided, and a bathroom was created, toilet, sink, bathtub with shower, and a closet. They put in a well and plumbed the house from bathroom to kitchen, even adding deep sinks in the basement.

Swanson's idea of a bathroom closet was first-cousin to a cave. A door, dead center between the end walls, created tunnels on each side that stretched to the room's outside walls where closet rods spanned each end of the openings. The result was a space about two feet wide into which garments were crammed to hang on either end of the five-foot deep tunnels. Where's that darned Asthmador?

Grandpa had been living in the city for the past 26 years and must have felt liberated moving to the island. I think he was finally happy again. He had settled into the island house, which was now shared with his son's family, and he had land to care for and home improvements to plan.

Imagine his joy at lighting the fuse and backing away a safe distance before the dynamite blew.

He died that winter.

* * *

I learned from my cousin Bosse that Grandpa Swanson was the second child born to Sven Petter Nilsson and Josefina Mathilda Nilsdotter. There would be eight to follow, all born in Kristdala, Sweden. Two of his brothers and one sister would immigrate to America, marry, and raise families.

Under an avalanche of information, I learned that in 1896, Grandpa's older brother and firstborn, Sven August Herman, was the first to come, settling and finding work in Rock Island, Illinois, a favorite destination for Swedes at the turn of the century.

Grandpa joined him in 1903 at the age of twenty-six.

Three years later, Sven August Herman married Anna Louise Franke, and they started their family in Rock Island, offering their home as the jumping-off point for sister Ester Alfinda Elizabeth and youngest brother Gustaf Adolf.

Ester would go on to marry Martin Tillberg and start a family in Wisconsin. I have had newly discovered cousins from that marriage spend the night at our house where we jabbered, exchanging stories and examining photos into the wee hours.

Sven August Herman moved his growing family to Wisconsin, as well. By 1930, he went by the name of Herman, and they had moved to California where they raised their family, and where I discovered a large number of cousins living today.

There was one brother that remained a puzzle. Even with his twenty-five years of research experience, Bosse had run into a dead-end trying to track down the youngest son, Gustaf Adolf Swanson, the last family member to immigrate.

Born June 7, 1889, the 1909 manifest of the ship he took to America, SS Lusitania, lists his destination as Rock Island, Illinois, where his brother Herman, lived at 2837 6th Avenue. He was nineteen at the time. He next appears in the 1920 census as living next-door to Herman's family in Wisconsin and is listed as an alien. From there, he seems to vanish without a trace.

It's a funny thing about photo albums and assorted memorabilia. Something that seems meaningless can offer a precious clue into a family's past. Pictures of faces that mean nothing to you suddenly take on immense significance when linked to another tidbit uncovered during your search and small pieces of paper with names that appear as gibberish can offer a priceless clue.

That's what happened with Gustaf.

Among other attributes, my mother was a selective saver. She rarely wrote on the backs of photos, preferring to lump them all into an extra thick cardboard box from Montgomery Ward. That box was a treasure trove of past picnics and family get-togethers; however, never a clue as to who was in the pictures. She also stashed legal documents, old letters, and bits of paper that were of special interest to her, thereby of irreplaceable value to me.

Of equal importance, were my grandmothers' picture albums? Both Granny Johnson and Grandma Swanson saved meaningful photos in albums, once again with no identification on the backs. I even found a couple of tintypes amongst the pictures of people from the old country. Rest assured, all of the pictures are in a safe place until another clue can shed light on the identities of the subjects.

In my search for Gustav Adolf's history, I remembered something I had found once in a tin box containing letters and legal documents. Included was a small, shirt pocket notebook with names, some recognized and some not, each followed by an abbreviated address. With the mere recognition of its existence, I placed it back into the box.

In my search for Gustav Adolf's history, I remembered that notebook, and after digging it out, alarms went off in my head when I read the eighth entry in my grandfather's hand, "G.A. Swanson…Gerry, NY RR1." In addition, my mother had saved a document from an attorney in Jamestown, New York, Gerry's county seat, regarding the settlement of the estate of one Gust Swanson. The executor of the estate was J. Pearl Swanson.

With those clues in hand, I began my online search for any history of a Swede by the name of Gust Swanson, living in Gerry, New York, while Grandpa was alive. Evidently, Gerry was a magnet for Swedes because there were several residents with that name.

Following fragmentary leads, I uncovered a cemetery inscription for G. Swanson on the Internet that listed the organization and individual responsible for recording and posting data from that cemetery. After placing a phone call, I was advised to contact the local paper. I attempted to do so and learned they had gone out of business years earlier. My contact encouraged me to get in touch with the Pendergrast Library, where archives from the defunct paper were kept. I drafted a letter of inquiry to the library as follows:

I am Dale Swanson, 68 years old, and am searching for a family member. His name was Gustav/Gustaf/Gust—Adolph/Adolf—Swanson. I believe he lived in Ellington and died on or about April 19, 1949. He was born June 7, 1889, in Kristdala, Sweden, and emigrated June 6, 1909, to Rock Island, Illinois. I have a scratchpad from my grandfather (his brother), which indicates he lived in Gerry/Ellington in the late 1940s. I believe he is buried in the Valley View Cemetery. I have no information telling me he was married, but my parents received notification from Jamestown regarding his estate. It was originated by J. Pearl Swanson. I believe he was married to J. Pearl, who died in 1966. The legal papers identified him as Gust Swanson, and I expect his obituary to be under that name. In addition to learning the specificity of his death, I am trying to determine if he had children. If so, they are lost to the family. Any help you can give me will be received with gratitude. I would greatly appreciate contact, whether positive or negative, as applies to your ability to help me.

Then I waited.

A few weeks later, I received a reply in the mail from the library. With letter in hand, I rushed into the house, waving it over my head, and excitedly yelled, "I got a reply from the library in New York!"

I ripped open the envelope, and inside was a photocopy of the short article from the newspaper.

My breath caught in my throat as I read the bold heading:

"FARMER FOUND HANGING SAID SUICIDE VICTIM—A verdict of suicide was issued Tuesday morning by Coroner Samuel T. Bowers after Gust A. Swanson, 59, of Ellington, was found hanging from a rope about 10:30 A.M. in the hayloft of his barn on the Ellington-Gerry Road..."

It went on to give more details, but my reeling mind couldn't get past the large print. What could have happened to make him end his life in this fashion? Although I didn't know him, I mourned his death and wondered if he had children. None were mentioned in the article that seemed to serve as his obituary. I intend to resume my search into his life and death, but for now, that research is taking a back seat to other projects. I hope to find out if there are other cousins to add to our growing family tree.

CHAPTER 2

Settling In

I have the good fortune of claiming two sisters: Jill, five-years older, Linda, five-years younger. When I was forming memories at ten, Jill, at fifteen, was very much involved with friends her age, and Linda was simply my little sister with her dolls and five-year-old friends. As children, we spent our days doing separate things, coming together during the dinner hour, family outings, and holiday celebrations. The age difference, coupled with the typical boy-girl relationships as kids, resulted in near separate childhoods and very different memories. Nevertheless, the extraordinary times in which we lived saw huge strides in technology taking place almost daily, giving us a common bond beyond that of the family unit.

Undoubtedly skewed by time and mental fog, my reflections of the goodness and innocence of growing up are a constant reminder of where I came from, and how my life was intrinsically and forever linked to Island Park and the joys of being a kid.

* * *

I took each of the worn pine steps leading to our basement carefully and slowly, finally stopping at the point where he became visible through the open

17

side and planted my rear end. I was nine. Moments earlier, my mother's message was, "Your father wants to see you."

He was in his small work area, hardly large enough to call a shop, working on a contraption that looked like a nightmare of black metal needles, ends hooked, and situated vertically on the outside of a black cylinder. There was a crank on one side, function unknown to me. He spoke without looking up from his work.

"I heard you and Larry were yelling unkind remarks at Mr. and Mrs. Wilson. Is it true?"

My breathing became ragged. How did he know? It couldn't have been ten minutes since we'd flung insults at the aging couple from behind Johnny's garage; loudly shouted words that to a nine-year-old were clever and daring.

"DRUNKARD. Have another beer. DRUNKARD, DRUNKARD."

The old man was attempting to back into his driveway, which was straight as a plumb line, but he couldn't keep the car online, getting out and walking unsteadily to the rear every so often to learn he failed; returning behind the wheel just as unsteadily to try it again. Mrs. Wilson, oblivious, sat in the passenger seat. After about four attempts, we started our chants.

My father, at last, turned away from his work and approached the stairs. Placing his hand on one of the steps, he looked directly into my eyes, waiting for an answer.

Tears began to well. "Yeah, dad, we did."

"How do you suppose that made them feel?"

Now the crying began in earnest. I was filled with remorse, not for what we had done, but because I had disappointed my dad.

I wanted to be like him. He was Santa Claus at the Island Park community Christmas party. He called Bingo at the annual Fireman's Field Days. He was the scoutmaster for Troop 201 before and after I was old enough to join. Moreover, he always had time for me. He proudly went to work each day as the custodian at Shirley Hills Elementary School, and he gave us everything we needed.

His discipline was a look, a softly stated question, an unspoken promise to teach right from wrong through example, and deep respect for others.

Mom and Dad on their Wedding Day

Mom and Dad married on June 29, 1935, and like millions of new-lyweds, they worked their way through hard times without knowing they were hard times. Youth, with its feeling of immortality coupled with the bliss accompanying their burgeoning love affair, rendered their peripheral problems as secondary.

The depression years of the '30s were tough on everyone, and my parents were no exception. Dad quit high school in 1929 to earn some money, and was hired as a knitter's helper at the Strutwear Knitting Company, 1015 South 6th street, Minneapolis.

Strutwear was a major player in the knitting industry and strongly anti-union. The company was a family business owned by the Struthers family, and their strong anti-labor stance helped make Minneapolis the focal point for the national labor movement. The knitters union went on strike in August 1935, on the heels of the truckers strike of 1934. Both were a big deal with local authorities, seemingly on the side of management. Police, and even National Guard troops were called out to maintain order, and there were many injuries and even deaths during the strikes.

After eight months, management conceded, demands were met, and the strike ended. The Struthers family would have the final word when they moved the company out of the state in 1953. I can only imagine the discussions that took place between Mom and Dad, centering on a job offer to relocate with the company. I'm sure both sides had their preference, stay, or move, but they agreed on a course of action and worked together to meet the challenge.

* * *

It was barely the second month of the year 1947 when grandpa died, and at the age of thirty-two Dad found himself responsible for his mother, his wife, and his two children, in a turn of the century summer home recently retrofitted with running water, a new bathroom, and little more. To top it off, he worked in Minneapolis, an hour's drive away.

The house was heated with a coal-burning furnace. My first impression of this behemoth was that of a comic book villain. The large cylinder that held the firebox reached nearly to the ceiling and was wrapped in a thick coating of asbestos. Near the top, meandering tentacles, also wrapped, disappeared into the darkness between floor joists, supposedly connecting to the heat registers in the floor above.

They delivered the coal through an opening into an area at the front of the house under the porch, which was separated from the remainder of the basement by a substantial foundation wall through which an opening was cut, and a door placed. When necessary, Dad moved smaller amounts of coal from the large pile in the delivery area to a spot more easily accessed from which he fed the furnace—specifically, a boxed-in area under the basement stairs. The fire was stoked and coal added by shoveling it through the furnace door, not unlike the process of feeding the fire in a steam locomotive.

I remember sitting on the stairs and watching Dad don heavy gloves, open the furnace door, and shovel coal into the inferno.

Swanson, the carpenter, stayed with us through the summer of '47, and the six of us fell into a routine. Mom's role was to care for the kids, wash clothes, keep the house, and argue with Swanson. Grandma did the cooking, and Dad worked at Strutwear during the day and on the house in the evenings.

They built a room off the back of the house, and it ran the entire width of the original house. It would become what we referred to as the amusement room. For the finale of Swanson's time with us, he and Dad framed in another bedroom above the amusement room, directly behind, but attached to the kitchen. I remember sitting on the cold boards in late autumn as Dad nailed them in place. This room would be Grandma's bedroom.

Grandma Swanson provided another twist in my efforts to tie family history together. My sisters and I knew she had three siblings, two sisters, and a brother. We went on summer picnics to "Aunt Dora's" house in Red Wing, where I remember waiting impatiently in front of the TV set watching the test pattern until the daily broadcasts began.

"Aunt Alma," lived with her husband, Swan, on fifty acres they owned outside the town of Cannon Falls. My memories of those picnics include walking the small bridge over the creek between the house and the barn and touching the tack for the horses Swan used to farm.

The men took me with them when they went up on the hill behind the house to shoot shotguns and tell stories. I remember Dad telling me about Dora's husband, Joey. It seems he was an excellent rifle shot when he was a young man, able to shoot coins out of the air. I saw for myself that he was a talker, and I was fascinated by his stories.

However, like Grandpa, Grandma's side of the family had a few things ripe for discovery.

My sisters and I knew nothing of her parents or the fact that she had an older brother and sister that we never knew. My Swedish cousin primed a pump that yielded countless discoveries of unknown ancestors, both paternal and maternal, each providing a glimpse into my family's past.

I learned that Grandma was confirmed in The Swedish Evangelical Church of Cannon Falls, in 1892, at the age of fourteen.

She was a young woman with movie star beauty when she spent time in Davenport, Iowa, in her early twenties. It was likely there that she met my grandfather, who immigrated to Rock Island, Illinois, in 1903. They married, and her life mirrored that of my grandfather until that horrible day of his death in February 1947.

Grandma moved into the back bedroom, and her life took on predictable tedium, broken only by family visits to her sisters in Red Wing and Cannon Falls.

As an adult, I wish I could have those years back; what a story she could have told. As a child, I appreciated none of it, and only now do I realize the loss.

Her quality of life began to spiral downward after the farm injury. Her beauty began to fade as a life that started with so much promise evolved into a lifetime of great sorrow and disappointments. She began to have bouts of unrelenting coughing, and on the evening of October 14, 1952, she was admitted to Glen Lake Tuberculosis Sanatorium, where she spent the last ten years of her life. She died in a nursing home on November 11, 1962.

I was in the US Navy, stationed in Karamursel, Turkey.

CHAPTER 3

Granny and Grandpa Johnson

M y grandpa on my mother's side, Olaf Conrad Johnson, was born in Eidsberg, Norway, in 1887. His birthplace is recorded as Brattefoss, translated as "Steep Waterfall." He emigrated in 1905, entering the United States through Canada.

Grandpa Olaf Conrad Johnson

Grandpa Johnson was a speed skater in the old country. With a thin build and long legs he likely excelled in that specific sport, although he seemed to love all winter activities. Growing up a short walk from the lake, I, like all my friends, had a pair of hockey skates, and my sister had her figure skates. I remember Grandpa's skates because of the long blade that extended far in front of the boot.

When he came to the U.S., he worked as a hired hand on Downing Farm in La Moure, North Dakota. With 125 head of horses, it was one of the largest farms in the area. I don't know when or why he left La Moure, and I'm not sure where he met my grandma, but a court commissioner married them in Minneapolis on December 26, 1913.

After they were married, he took a job as a packer in the red-hot flour milling industry. His employer was the Washburn Crosby Co.—later to become the Pillsbury Company—at Sixth Avenue South and First Street, Minneapolis.

The days were few when he didn't wear a suit and tie, topped off with a fedora worn at a confident angle. On the weekends, while not dressed in a formal manner, his trousers were always pressed and creased, and there was never a wrinkle in his shirts. He often wore a simple baseball cap when he dressed for the weekends. Thin and over six feet tall with an oval face and a forehead hairless as an egg, he was quiet and soft-spoken, a true gentleman.

He and Granny located to the island during the summer months. I'm sure the fact that his friend Einer Swenson lived there served as an extra impetus to move close to his daughter's family for the summer. The first house I remember them living in was on the corner directly across the road from Einer's place. A little later, I remember them in a small cottage, just three houses east of Einer's.

I loved having him close. He always had time to show interest in what I was doing, and on more than one occasion, he went skating with my friends and me. His skating came to an end when he fell and hit his head. Scared the daylight out of me, and that was the last time I would ever see him on the ice.

* * * *

Granny Anna Anderson/Johnson

While Grandpa Johnson was tall and thin, Granny could best be described as stout. She dressed in a conservative manner, in my mind's eye, I see her now in an ankle-length dress that buttons the whole length in the front, knitted lisle stockings reaching up to her knees. Her legs tapered evenly from knees to foot, with no definable calf muscles or shapely ankles. She wore her hosiery rolled halfway down. On her feet, she wore black shoes with an ample toe-box and a wide, raised heel. While on the go, she always had a purse hanging from her forearm.

Granny Johnson's life was anything but straightforward, and to understand her, we need to understand her past. She had two sisters who died before she was born, five surviving sisters, and a brother.

Her life in Norway must have been difficult. Her father owned a general store and was doing quite well until a lumber company came into the area. The company requested credit with a promise to pay when the lumber was sold. Taking advantage of his naiveté, they left the area without paying their bill, putting her father out of business, and placing the family into a precarious situation.

Granny's older sister, Mary, was the first to immigrate, accompanied by her younger brother Andrew. They landed in Boston in 1901. Mary ended up in Waupaca, Wisconsin, while Andrew lived out his life in Buck Lake, Manitoba, Canada.

In a letter from Mary's daughter, Elizabeth, we get a hint into the final years of Granny Johnson's father, Ole Anderson.

"Grandpa was twenty-two years older than Grandma, and he was blind for ten years. During this time, Grandma took complete care of him. Grandpa was a good Christian, and he spent days praying for his children in America. He would pray for one and then another over and over again. Grandma said he was in heaven more than he was on earth during the years he was blind."

Andrew, the black sheep of the family, could best be described as a Rounder. The only boy in the family, he was spoiled beyond measure and exhibited a self-serving nature for as long as he lived. His father died at the age of ninety-four, at which time his mother came to America to live with her daughter Mary, in Waupaca leaving the homestead called "Bolvik" to be sold by the solicitor.

In the same letter quoted above, Elizabeth best illustrates Andrew's character while speaking of his actions toward his mother, Gunhild.

"In Norway, when the home place was sold, and both parents deceased, the oldest son inherited the property. When Bolvik was sold, Andrew received the money. Andrew knew grandma (Gunhild) *needed her money from her home, but he never gave her a penny. Grandma wrote to him and asked him for her money. She never received a response. This made Grandma very sad. We lost all respect for Andrew after this."*

Granny Johnson was missing the tip of one of her fingers, thanks to Andrew. He was separating bullets from their casings and saving the gunpowder for blowing things up and other types of mischief. Granny was with him, and somehow the primer in a shell casing exploded, taking the tip of her finger.

My cousin, Terry, was likely the closest to Andrew. He visited him in his house in Buck Lake and stayed there for a summer, during which time Andrew regaled him with stories of life at the turn of the century in Manitoba, Canada. Andrew was quite a character and told of shooting a moose, quartering and hanging him in a tree, and lowering him to cut off a chunk when needed. He offered first-hand proof that shooting a charging grizzly between the eyes with a 30-30 bullet results in little more than confusing the bear as the bullets glance off his skull, and if you are lucky, it is possible to escape during his muddled state. He also convinced Terry that he found a rich vein of gold, but became lost during a sudden snowstorm and was unable to return to the same place.

His house was a one-room cabin heated by a wood stove and contained the barest necessities in furniture and cookware. The limited comforts might help explain his actions while he visited our house the only time I remember.

I watched him as he sat in our living room, talking to my dad. He was smoking a cigarette and casually flicking ashes on my mother's braided rug. He was lucky she didn't see him, or he would have wished he'd had his 30-30. His action was further explained when my parents visited him in Buck Lake, and he invited them into his one-room cabin, dirt floor, and all.

* * *

I don't remember ever seeing my grandparents show affection toward each other, always respectful, but never a hug. When Grandpa wanted to visit Norway, Granny refused to go with him. I don't think anyone understood the dynamics of their relationship, but she refused to go with him, electing to stay at home.

Grandpa's job at the flour mill paid well. That, coupled with the fact that Granny was an excellent money manager, allowed them the financial freedom to travel and do things many others could not afford.

In the early forties, O.T. Lee was the salesman for the J.R. Watkins Company, and Grandma and Grandpa's house was a regular stop on his route. My cousin Terry, seven years old in 1942, lived with Granny and Grandpa during that time and told the story this way:

> *"I used to love it when O.T. Lee came to the house, especially around Christmas time. Grandma and Grandpa welcomed him as a friend, and they shared a glass or two of Christmas wine while sitting around listening to his spiel. Then, when it was time for him to go, I'd run to the couch that butted against the front windows to watch the action. This was in the forties, and O.T. drove a Model T, you know the kind that you had to hand-crank to start. I'd watch him set the ignition, walk to the front, grab the crank, and give it a twist. He'd give it a few cranks until it finally caught.*
>
> *Lee, dressed as for a funeral, jumped to the side as the Model T lurched forward. With overcoat flapping, one hand on his hat, Lee grabbed the door handle and chased the car until he could jump on the running board and slide behind the wheel. It was a great show."*

CHAPTER 4

Irrepressible Older Sister

My older sister, Jill, has always had a strong personality, and even now, there is very little middle ground. Things are either black or white, right or wrong, my way or the hi-way. This led to adventures that bubble up in my memory that, with a little thought, glow with the luster of gold. She always had something rattling around in her bean that turns out to be a gem when uncovered and dusted off sixty years later. Jill was blessed with a bottomless reservoir of schemes for making an honest buck. I can only guess at the patience that Mom had to have while putting up with, and sometimes assisting in, *Productions By Jill.*

While going through a stack of old pictures, I was reintroduced to one of these jewels from the past. I held in my hand a photo of neighbor and co-conspirator, Joyce Moore, and sister Jill flanking Joyce's little brother Jerry, who was about three at the time. They were on the sidewalk leading to Moore's house. Poor Jerry, duped, no doubt, into joining the girls in play wearing a befuddled expression as the girls each held a hand. In the middle stands Jerry, with all the accouterments of a baby doll; frilly dress, bonnet somewhat askew, and ribbons meant to tie under the chin hanging loosely on each side of his round head.

Jill was writer, star, producer, and director of epic plays staged in the horse shed behind our house. She also served as set designer and publicist, dispensing flyers to all the neighbors announcing the latest offering. On the shed's double doors, she displayed her talents as sign painter by painting in capital letters, "Saturday Playhouse."

Inside, she hung flowered curtains at the single window to the right of the doors; and the stage, at the same level as the shed floor, was given prominence through a sheet that hung as a curtain to separate actors from the audience until slid to one side.

I have no recollection of any attempts to commercialize Easter or Christmas, but Halloween brought out her best. For this production, she needed the relative shelter offered by the backside of the basement in what the family referred to as the recreation room. There, she set her "Walk of Horror." After payment of a few cents, the customer was blindfolded and led through a string of items culled from mom's pantry to represent grotesque and distorted body parts identifiable by touch alone.

There was a brain molded from Jell-o, and grape eyeballs suspended in bodily fluids of tapioca pudding. She had stockings stuffed with whatever was handy and immersed them in warm, undiluted tomato soup, which was presented as entrails of a dog. Everything she had was in some kind of fluid with varying viscosities. She had wiener fingers suspended in boiled macaroni, and slimed up cantaloupe skulls with hollows for eyes and nose. Her imagination knew no bounds as she led each customer through the chamber of horrors, describing the contents of each bowl and how it happened to be there, as tentative fingers probed the unknown.

* * *

After Dad's brother, Uncle Stanley, died, and my aunt moved her family to Rapid City, Mom and Dad invited their daughters, Sue, Gwen, and Bonnie, to our place for the summers. Gwen was the oldest, followed by Susan, and then Bonnie. Gwen was always the responsible one. Two years older than Jill, her younger sisters looked to her as the go-to person when their mom was absent. This meant that Gwen was in charge when they took the Greyhound bus from Rapid City to Minneapolis. Once the cousins set foot on the island, Jill was the source for most of the ideas that coupled together like so many boxcars to make each summer special.

As the years passed and the girls became teenagers, Mom and Dad began to figure more prominently into the summertime equation. Jill was attractive; Gwen had the look of Swedish innocence, broad cheekbones, and freckled nose, blond pigtails poking out each side of her head; Susan was a duplicate of Jill, blond hair and oval face; and Bonnie was as cute as a button. The boys flocked to the house. Dad likely oiled up the shotgun, and Mom donned the warden's hat.

As for me, I was in seventh heaven. Even at that early age, I knew cute girls when I saw them, and I studied the moxie the boys brought to the house; the wrestling matches in the front yard and general commotion as they stumbled to impress. They put up with me as the "little brother," and I made the most of it until Jill shooed me away.

During the same period that my Rapid City cousins came to our house in the summer, something happened that would strain Mom and Dad's pocketbook and highlight their sense of responsibility toward friends as well as family.

Dad had a good friend named Patrick O'Connor. Pat lived in Minneapolis with his wife and two young boys. Dad and Pat were deer hunting in north-central Minnesota. It was mid-November, and the weather was chilly with a fresh snowfall on the ground. They were hunting in separate areas when Dad heard a shot from Pat's direction. Figuring he shot a deer, he headed that way only to find Pat lying in a heap.

Patrick O'Connor died that day, the recipient of another hunter's bullet. The person who pulled the trigger and ended a life, never stepped forward to take responsibility for what had been done, and Dad never hunted deer again. However, for the next two or three years, we entertained Pat's two boys for a couple of weeks each summer, and Dad drove into Minneapolis on multiple occasions to help Pat's wife when things around the house needed fixing.

I'll never know which of my parents insisted on giving of themselves to help others, and I guess it doesn't matter who's idea it was. They were givers, and the world has too few of them. The things I saw while a child was the product of two people finding common ground and acting together to achieve a goal. I am forever grateful for the lesson.

CHAPTER 5

The Early Years

On February 17, 1948, my younger sister Linda was born. A few things stand out in my mind about that day. My main thought was why the heck did Mom have to go to the hospital to meet the stork that was bringing our new baby? Seems like it made a lot more sense if he'd just fly to our house directly.

I remember when she left. I knew I would miss her, and I looked forward to her return with a brand new baby as much as I looked forward to Christmas. That night I came out of the bedroom after hearing someone in the living room, and there in the dim light, I saw the silhouette of Mom walking toward me. My heart jumped to my throat as I dashed toward her and flung my arms around her legs.

"Well, that's quite a greeting."

What? This isn't Mom. That's not Mom's voice. It sure isn't Grandma Swanson. I stepped away, confused and embarrassed.

"Dale Baby. I'll be here for the next several days." Granny Johnson was the only one to call me "Dale Baby."

"Where's my mom? Is she coming home with my new baby?"

"Yes, everything is fine. We have to wait until the stork comes, and your mom thought I could keep you company while we wait together. Your dad has to go to work, you know."

When Mom finally came home, she was carrying a small bundle. That was my initiation into the life of my sister Linda. Impossibly tiny, I was allowed to gently cradle her in my arms only if I was sitting in a chair. I knew she was something special.

* * *

I attended second grade in the Island Park Community Church. The church was in the process of being built, so, in concert with the times, the basement was finished first with the roof destined to become the floor for the church proper. The rear wall was dug into a hillside while the entrance was through a door leading to stairs that delivered us to the basement church.

Once inside, there was a divider running the length of the rectangle to divide the space into two rooms. The divider collapsed like an accordion to allow church services or other functions requiring the larger area. Upon entering, to the left, services were held, to the right, a wall enclosed a cloakroom. The cloakroom was where disciplinary problems were worked out. A disruptive student was sentenced to do time in isolation, duration dependent upon the severity of the disruption. I think I may hold the record for cloakroom time.

Our second-grade teacher, who I really don't remember, likely carried memories of my second-grade class for her entire life. Unfortunately, I doubt they were good memories, because of what happened one fall day.

Several weeks earlier, she had arranged a field trip for the class. It was to be the culmination of our study of dairy cows, and we looked forward to our trip to the dairy in Maple Plain with unbridled excitement.

As the day wore on, class behavior deteriorated. Apparently, my behavior had something to do with that deterioration. I remember hiding under the teacher's desk with no recollection of how or why I got there. For some reason, my seven-year-old mind figured I was safe there, and pretty much immune from authority. The problem was, at the time I crawled under the teacher's desk, I had forgotten about the field trip.

"Come out of there this instant."

She can't be talking to me. I'm invisible.

"Dale, get out here right now, and I'm not kidding."

No answer.

Finally, in frustration, class itching to get going, my teacher delegated responsibility to her counterpart on the other side of the divider. After a brief discussion, they slid back the curtain for unfettered visibility, and I was told in no uncertain terms that when I decided to come out from under the desk, I was to stand in the cloakroom until they returned.

This was a great insult. After all, I had looked forward to going to the dairy ever since she told us about the trip. The class left, and twenty minutes of mulling my predicament from under the desk and realizing the unjust punishment, I made a break for it. Darting into the cloakroom, while the alternate teacher's back was turned, I grabbed my knit cap, the one that fit me like a helmet and buttoned under my chin, snatched my jacket off the hook, and bounded up the stairs.

Years later, as an adult, I heard about the episode from my mother's perspective.

"I was at the kitchen sink, looking out the window, and I saw this little kid walking up the road kicking rocks. Then I realized it was you.

"What are you doing home at this hour?"

"I left."

"You left? What do you mean? You left?"

"I dunno. I just left."

"Did the teacher send you home?"

"Yeah. Teacher sent me home."

"Why?"

"She couldn't get me out from under the desk."

"What?"

"She couldn't get me out from under the desk."

"Why were you under the desk?"

"I crawled under?"

"What? Why did you crawl under?"

"I dunno. She was gonna make me go to the cloakroom."

"Gonna make you . . . Why was she sending you to the cloakroom?"

"I dunno. I guess she was mad at me."

"Why was she mad at you?"

"I dunno. Ma, can I have some toast?"

"You go to your room."

So—I went to my bedroom and wondered what I did wrong.

Sometime later, Mom called me into the living room.

"Put on your jacket. We're going back to school."

I put my jacket on, and she slapped the cap on my head, buttoning the strap under my chin, put my little sister, Linda, into her stroller, and off we went. To say I was worried would be an understatement.

When we arrived in front of the church/school, Mom stationed Linda in the park across the road, and I was instructed to wait with her while she went inside. Today she would be arrested for that, but in 1949, in the Village of Island Park, Linda and I were as safe as if in a neighbors yard. Shortly after she entered, the class, back from the dairy, was excused for recess. Oh, boy! Scared to death for the questions and teasing I was about to get, I hid behind Linda's stroller.

That's my last remembrance of the episode, although I'm pretty sure I spent the rest of the day in the cloakroom and my conduct likely improved, at least for a week or two, however, most of my early school report cards made reference to poor study habits, wasted potential, and incessant poking and prodding of fellow students.

I wasn't mean, just poking, prodding, teasing, and annoying my peers.

* * *

Mid August was the time that wild grapes, apples, and pears could be eaten, although not yet fully ripe. We set up raids on neighboring apple trees and Einer Swenson's lone pear tree. Green apple raids, in spite of the severe bellyaches aples caused, were our favorite. One of the problems with green apples was that the pain could follow the eating by several hours. Two or three apples would cause half an hour of absolute misery, and five or six made you wish for a quick death. Once the pain began, it grew exponentially: The greater the number of apples, the longer the pain.

"Dale. Were you eating green apples?"

"Naw, Mom." Absolute denial.

"Are you sure you weren't eating green apples?"

"Yeah, Ma, I'm sure."

"I'm going to call the doctor. This has been going on too long."

The family doctor diagnosed it as appendicitis and had me admitted to the hospital. The Emergency Room nurse pushed on my abdomen.

"Does that hurt?"

"Ouch, yes!"

"Does that?"

"Oww, oww, oww!"

By the time the doctor arrived, they had prepped me for surgery. I was lying on the gurney, attendants pawing the floor with their tennis shoes aching to race me into the operating room. The doctor poked, and the pain was gone.

"Nothing?"

"No."

"How about here?"

"No."

"Here?"

"A little."

"Here?"

"No."

"Alright—what have you been eating?"

"Nothin.—Ma, what have I been eatin?"

I saw her eyes narrow, face turn from concern to suspicion, and a clear indication of mounting anger.

"Dale . . . did you eat green apples today?"

"No, Ma!"

"Dale!"

"Well, maybe a little."

A switch was flicked.

"How many apples?"

"Just a couple. Ma, I only had a couple."

"Dale! How many?"

"Well, maybe three."

"How many!"

"About three, I think."

"Oh. Only three?" Her eyes transferred toward the doctor. "Doctor . . . I've seen him after three apples. There's more here than a green apple bellyache. You'd better go ahead and operate."

"What're they gonna do, Ma?"

The doctor, sensing where this was heading, approached with a serious countenance.

"We're going to roll you through that door and cut you open. Who knows, we might find nothing and just sew you back up. No big deal. A few months and you'll be back to normal."

Gulp. "Ma . . . what if I had more than three?"

"How many more?"

"What if I ate six or seven?"

I don't remember the discipline, but it was clearly deserved.

* * *

One of my earliest buddies and long-term resident of the island was Donnie Bryce. The two of us shared our school lives from first grade through graduation from high school. Donnie is gone now, called home to God, but I'm happy to say I still count him as a friend. His father, Nick, was my Sunday school teacher and a wonderful man who was the first to kindle my interest in being a Christian, but at seven years old, there was a big difference between Sunday school and church.

Although only seven, I already looked forward to weekends. Saturdays were the best day of the week, with Sundays a close second, although set aside for family activities, limiting our free time. Weekends were what we lived for, not counting summer vacation. The only clinker in the weekend was church on Sundays. Church meant sitting through the sermon. Sitting still for anything was an enormous task, especially when there were other kids forced into the same predicament. Our parents learned early on to separate us by at least two rows of chairs.

Any time we found ourselves within reach of another kid, it was impossible to keep from finding a way to agitate. All it took was a foot to nudge the other's chair, or a spitball flicked with the thumb. Most times, we just made faces at each other. Nobody's parents dared smack the transgressor during the service, so Mom's preferred method of discipline followed a prescribed sequence: without taking her eyes off the preacher, and maintaining a heavenly, angelic look on her face, she gently and slowly reached out, grabbed my arm in a viselike grip, and dug in manicured nails.

Her meaning was crystal clear. Cut it out, now!

No matter the season, church was a requirement on Sundays. During the summer, on days when it wasn't raining, we walked. When it was raining, we piled into Dad's car and rode.

The onslaught of winter was usually a gradual event. In late October, puddles, frozen overnight, refused to melt, and the ruts on the gravel roads turned solid, threatening to twist the ankle of the inattentive. As October passed and the days moved deep into November, there were occasional episodes of light snow that blew into the ruts and hid the ice on the frozen puddles. By early December, the bright colors of summer were a memory, and autumn's red and crimson became gray and muted.

After winter arrived, we took the car every Sunday.

After the services ended, the grownups often socialized over coffee. I imagine that after a week of relative confinement in separate homes, a touch of cabin fever would begin to set in, and they relished the adult company. The final "amen" meant something altogether different to us kids. To me, it meant the end of my weekly obligation. I was now free to play! Although we weren't permitted to roam off church property, there was no shortage of imagination in the class of second graders when it came to finding trouble. King-of-the-hill was a staple, and we wrestled and pushed each other down the slope leading to the road, each of us doing everything we could to achieve Alpha Male status.

Usually, a snowball to the face was enough to put a damper on the fun, at which point the transgressor was hauled back into the basement and forced to apologize to the recipient.

One morning after the service, we shrugged into our winter coats and charged up the stairs, anxious to escape to the Neverland of continuous play. We had snow the night before, so everything was white and clean as we poured from the building.

We weren't outside for five minutes before we found it tucked behind a bush at the edge of the building.

"Hey...whose sled?"

"Sled?"

"Yeah, someone left a sled here."

Donnie grabbed the thing and made a dash for the hill. Plopping on his stomach, he sped down the slope, intending to launch off the snowbank left from earlier plowings and skid to a stop on the icy road.

"Donnie!"

He didn't hear me yell his name.

"Donnie, Donnie. Stop, stop, stop!"

Runners cutting through fresh snow on top of crusted ice make more noise than you'd think. He didn't hear a word.

By then, everyone else was waving arms and yelling at the top of their lungs.

Rounding the bend and heading our way, Al Boll was making his first pass at clearing the fresh snow. It flew from the plow blade as Al sat back in the driver's seat, confident in his contribution to the good of all.

It was clear that Donnie was oblivious to the danger—and Boll wasn't slowing.

Somehow, Boll saw him moments before the sled cleared the bank, and he hit the brakes hard. Donnie twisted to his right and disappeared under the avalanche. The truck, wheels locked, skidded to a stop on the packed snow.

"Donnie. Donnie."

Girls were screaming. I stood there unbelieving, mesmerized by the scene, as the cadre charged down the hill. Donnie was nowhere in sight, and I dared not think of what just happened.

Al came around the back of the truck and approached the plow. He dropped to his knees and stuffed his upper body into the opening between the front wheel and the plow blade. His legs thrashed as he scrambled as far as he could into the narrow opening. He stayed there for perhaps a minute, backed out to reposition, and crawled under the truck behind the front wheel. More squirming and flailing of legs until he scampered from underneath and again dove into the crease between the plow and wheel. Another couple of minutes and he inched his way from under the vehicle, Donnie in tow.

I don't remember the extent of his injuries or whether there were any injuries at all. I don't recall an adult presence beyond that of Al Boll, although I'm sure they rushed from the church. The bottom line; the episode was implanted and remains vivid in my mind.

Although I was unaware of it at the time, this would be the first of many stupid risks I would see, or participate in, during my sixty-plus years. With the advantage of hindsight, I am a firm believer that the male mind is slow to mature, which dovetails nicely with the fact that we play second fiddle to our woman of choice for our entire lives.

After all, they've had at least fifteen years' head start at perfecting the art of living a mature life.

CHAPTER 6

The Neighborhood

Just as in the "Our Gang" comedies with Alfalfa, Spanky, Buckwheat, and the others, I had neighborhood friends who lived for adventure and mischief. Our episodes seldom included all of us at once, but in groups of two, three and four, we went on big game hunts, stormed castles, swung on vines, and punched cattle; we fought Indians and fought wars; we acted out our comic book inspired fantasies with little more than our imaginations.

FRONT: Me, Dickey Moore, Darlene Bursch, Betsy Bursch
REAR: Larry Bursch (hiding), Leroy (Skeeter) Bursch, Jill Swanson

We'd play all sorts of games. When we played war, which was quite often, I was Audie Murphy, the Medal of Honor winner from World War II.

When we played cowboys, although I idolized Little Beaver, I had a-hankerin' to be Roy Rogers, partly because he was another of my heroes, but just as much because it gave me the rights to Trigger.

Trigger was by far the smartest horse alive. I can remember standing in front of Mom's bedroom mirror practicing my draw. Whew, I was fast. Between my prowess with a cap gun and Trigger to outrun anything the west had to offer, I figured I was just about invincible.

Then there was the dump! We probably spent way too much time in the local dump picking stuff that was perfect for our inventions: pieces of metal, old shoes, springs of every imaginable configuration, casters from discarded chairs. Each brought excitement as we explored the possibilities of the find. I even brought home, with the help of Johnny and Larry, an old banister that we were convinced was perfect for our next fort. Of course, our parents ended up returning the items to the heaping pile of discarded junk after our interest waned and it was time to rid the house of useless trash.

Our gang consisted of kids who lived in about a three-block area that ran down the hill in front of our house to the west. Moving down the hill toward the Village Hall, the closest house was Larry's. Larry was my best buddy and partner in most of my adventures.

One more house and a low stretch of narrow swamp later was George Farnham's house. George was a little older than I and had a serious countenance about him. I remember he had two sisters named Beatrice and Roberta. I don't ever remember seeing George's mother outside the house, but his father was a daily occurrence as he walked the road from his home, up the hill past ours, and on toward Avalon where he would catch a bus to take him to work in Minneapolis. He seemed to be very old and walked with a slight limp, head tilted toward the ground with apparent disinterest toward left or right. At the end of every day, the process was reversed.

I remember their house as being almost square with a center entry into the living room and an upright piano against the inside wall. Roberta, at the time, seemed like an excellent pianist. I seem to have a remembrance of George playing the bassoon at one time or another, but if memory serves, his instrument of choice was the trombone.

George's family seemed a serious lot, nose to the grindstone, make-something-of-your-life serious, and George was an excellent student. His senior graduating class voted him Most Talented.

Just past George's was where Johnny Storke lived. Johnny was an only child. He was one year younger than I, husky with a round, good-looking face, always with a quick smile and contagious laugh. I don't remember him as ever being afraid. He refrained from following us on our most stupid dares, but not because he was afraid. I'm convinced he was blessed with more common sense than the rest of us. And he was a strong kid. Not the least bit spoiled, Johnny was probably my second best friend. His dad, Kenny, was of average height, muscular, and endowed with the coordination of an athlete. I've seen him race out the front door in house slippers, leap onto the road, and race to the Village Hall where the fire trucks were garaged, in less than a minute. He served as constable for Island Park, and everyone knew he wasn't to be provoked.

Johnny's mom, Marion, was a natural beauty. It must have run in the family, because her sisters, Joyce and Ruby, were also knockouts. Get the three of them together, and heads would turn. Get the three of them together sunbathing in the front yard and cars would nearly run off the gravel as drivers forgot about watching the road.

I pictured Kenny and Marion as the quintessential homecoming king and queen.

One time, Johnny and I were in his room going through our comic collections with trading in mind. Somehow, Marion learned that I had a book of matches in my jeans pocket.

"Give me those matches Dale."

"What matches?"

"You rascal; give them to me."

"I ain't got no matches."

She made a move to grab me, and I squirmed away, dashed into their bedroom, and dove under the bed.

"C'mon. Crawl out of there this instant and give me the matches."

Maybe if I ignore her, she'll go away.

"Dale. That's enough. Just give me the matches."

Don't say a word. Just lie still. What's this? She's leaving the room.

Sure enough, Johnny's mom was just standing at the doorway.

What's this? Oh no, she got help!

"Ruby, you go around the other side. We'll get him."

Oh, crap. I'm a dead man.

I squirmed and wiggled to avoid the arms reaching for me as Johnny's mom and his Aunt Ruby giggled and strategized on ways to get me into their clutches. I don't recall how it turned out, but the memory of me under that bed and the two of them trying to grab me is pretty vivid.

Next to Johnny's was Einer Swenson's house. Einer worked with Grandpa Johnson at one of the flour mills in Minneapolis, and from stories I heard, he was an active union organizer during the labor movement of the early thirties. Einer and Amy Swenson were real jewels, Einer, the bigger than life Norwegian, and Amy, his quiet, unassuming rock. I loved them both. They had two kids: Sherman, a tall, thin, intellectual type, and Dickey, much shorter, much heavier, and far less devoted to his education. Sherman was at least six years my senior, and Dickey was a couple of years older than me. Neither was a member of our close-knit group.

Next in line was Al and Jenny Boll's house, across the street from the Village Hall, the fire barn, and the handful of buildings used to store the island's maintenance trucks and equipment. Boll also had an icehouse for storing block ice through the summer. They had quite a few children: Donnie, Marlys, Rick, Doug, and Anne. One brother died in a construction accident. Of the two brothers that bracketed me, Rick was older, and we seldom played together. Doug, who was younger, joined us more often but wasn't a core member of the gang.

Across the road from Boll's was where Ronnie Hart lived. I'm forced to use a pseudonym because Ronnie was likely the most cream puff person I ever met as a kid. As every football team has a star, each gang of kids has a Ronnie; loyal to a fault, well-liked by all but just not up to par when it came to the physical aspects of our agenda; he was white as Casper, perpetually sunburned in July, with a constant sinus infection year-round. He was a friend for as long as I knew him.

Right across the street from me, lived Dickey Moore.

Dickey was two years older, and much more talented than I. His Dad worked for the railroad and sometimes was gone for days at a time. There were four kids in the Moore family, and he was the oldest boy. Dickey was one of those guys with natural athletic abilities, and he was the oldest of my playmates. It didn't matter what game we were playing, he ran faster, climbed higher, jumped farther, threw straighter, and rode his bike with more reckless abandon than anyone in the neighborhood. He could also shoot a slingshot better than I.

* * *

"Thunk!" The empty can disappeared behind the stump.

"Nice shot." I circled to the left trying to locate the can. I had two rocks left, and didn't want to end this game without a hit of my own.

There it sat, strangely upright, a massive dent in the side. I aimed, positioning the can in my line of sight dead center between the forks and stretched the bands to their limit, eyes fixed on the target.

When the concentration is focused, and everything is perfect, you know the instant you release that you have a good shot. You can feel it, the air, brushing the sides of the stone, swirling around the irregularities as it speeds toward the target. You can imagine the impact and anticipate the sound of contact. Everything is perfect.

I didn't get that feeling. I missed.

"Nice try." It was Dickey.

Nice TRY? I hate those two words.

"That was a bad rock." I knew darn well that the shape and size of the rock were perfect for my slingshot. "Watch this shot!"

"No, wait. Let's set it back on the stump, and we can have a duel."

Dickey and I played together a lot, and his athleticism could be a source of irritation. It didn't matter much to me whether I won or not, I just liked playing. In all actuality, I needed a win now and then to balance things out, and it was nearly impossible to win when Dickey was involved.

One time we were talking about cowboys, and I brought up Ken Maynard and his horse, Tarzan. We were amazed by the fact that all Ken had to do was whistle, and the loyal Tarzan would come a-runnin'. Well, I couldn't help but brag about the fact that my dog, Mike, did the same for me.

Dickey wasn't about to let me get away with that.

"Skipper comes when I whistle for her." Skipper was a small, long-haired mutt, all white except for black stockings and one black patch around her right eye. Skip was a sweet dog.

I was surprised, because I never saw Dickey whistle for Skipper, and we spent a lot of time together.

"Watch this if you don't believe me." Dickey slammed two fingers in his mouth and let out a powerful whistle.

Skipper, on the other side of the road, didn't notice a thing—just kept sniffing the bushes. Dickey clapped his hands together a couple of times and let out another whistle followed by the shout "Here, Skip!" Skip's head snapped in our direction. Dickey puffed up. I would have been nuts to point out the obvious, "Your dog came because you called his name," because Dickey could always beat me up, and I didn't enjoy being pummeled.

Anyway, that's how we got along. I would have loved to outshine Dickey at anything; I just hadn't done it yet.

"Let's set it back on the stump, and we can have a duel."

Oh, sure. I had never won a duel with Dickey. I had never come close to winning a duel with Dickey.

"Yeah, Okay."

Walking to pick up the can, I had a glimmer of an idea. What if I surprised Dickey? What if I got the advantage? Usually, our duels were fought like those in the movies except that we would walk side-by-side, spin around, and shoot at a stump or something.

This duel was different. The target was there, but Dickey wouldn't be pacing away, step-by-step, as in our regular duels. He was already at the maximum distance. I would be the only one walking away from the can. Facing the other direction, he had to rely on me to signal when to turn and shoot. I had control of the duel!

I placed the can on the stump. "OK. This is the game." I walked away from the stump.

I could see that Dickey didn't have a rock in his slingshot pocket. He didn't even have one out of his pants pocket! If I did things right, it was actually possible for me to get off the first shot. Should I cheat? My imagination began to perk. I could see my mother, tears running from her eyes, as she told my father the awful truth.

"Dale cheated today." My mother would sob.

"WHAT?"

"Dale cheated in a duel with Dickey today."

"NO, NOT MY SON DALE."

"He took half-steps in the duel."

After that, things would go downhill fast.

No, I had to give Dickey an equal chance. However, I didn't have to make it easy for him. Everything depended on my ability to keep his interest.

"We have to turn our backs to the target."

Dickey turned and stuck his hand into his pants pocket, searching for a rock. His superior manner was irritating, although well earned, and I could almost read his mind; "Here we go again. Ho-hum! Dale loses another duel."

I spoke slowly as I outlined the rules. Whatever I thought came out my mouth, which strangely, bolstered my confidence.

"I'll take five steps, then we both turn and shoot. If anyone turns before I take that fifth step, they're disqualified. Okay?"

Dickey didn't say a word.

"Agreed?"

"Yeah." I could see, from the corner of my eye, that he had turned his head with a slight cock in my direction. Was that uncertainty I saw in his eyes?

I looked at him, gave a slight nod, and began counting out loud with each pace.

"One—Two—Three." Dickey was still staring in my direction. "Four—Five."

I wheeled, drew the pocket, aimed, and released.

The can rocketed backward as Dickey's stone smacked into the stump. I HAD WON THE DUEL! Dickey was shouting, "Cheat...you cheated." I was elated. His yelling and claims of cheating wilted into the background. I had just won a duel against Dickey! Let him rave; I knew the truth. I won. I won.

He was still complaining when I picked up the can. Beaming, and with an unwarranted attitude, I sauntered in his direction, braggadocio paramount.

Not accustomed to second place, he did his best to dismiss the whole episode as an aberration. I, on the other hand, needled and gouged his self-esteem until he could take no more. Dickey's rage overflowed, and I found myself flat on my back with a handful of grass shoved in my face. My superior attitude disappeared, replaced with the more familiar runner-up mentality common to my daily regimen.

Eventually, he backed off, grabbed his slingshot, and headed for home.

That put an end to our companionship for a few hours, but we soon reconnected and looked for new challenges in new places just as though nothing had happened.

But something did happen. I beat Dickey for the first time in my life. Nothing would ever take that away, and a small change had taken place on my path to becoming an adult.

CHAPTER 7

Swamp Monsters

August was my favorite month of the year. I woke up in the mornings on the porch and realized I'd slept without covers the whole night, the temperature already comfortable when my eyes opened.

August. I loved the stillness of the air when the sun was high, the intense heat, and the sweat running off my forehead and down the bridge of my nose.

I loved not being cold.

The days were long and hot, and all the families seemed to look forward to the coolness of the evening hours. At twilight, the entire neighborhood came to life as people walked the gravel roads, stopping to visit along the way. Dad and the other men played horseshoe until it got too dark to see the stakes, and Mom entertained the neighbor ladies on the front porch.

Of course, the kids took advantage of the cool evenings too. We usually gathered at the top of the hill in front of our house to organize and play our evening games. With the familiar swamp close to the house, it was a natural for hide-n-seek.

Dad kept the hollow mowed to the edge of the swamp. The hollow was mostly open space while sporting a few apple trees, some oaks, and two beautiful birches. He loved working outside and took pride in keeping it as neat as any city park. One summer, on a warm Sunday, a car pulled onto the grass at the top of the hollow, and a family spread a blanket and had a picnic. He never said anything to them, proud that they thought it was a park.

The hollow had a definite line where the grass, made soft by Dad's mowing, met the un-mowed swamp. The swamp grass was waist high, and when dry, made a perfect hide-n-seek spot. Larry and I considered each other as professional hiders.

* * *

"1, 2, 3, 4, 5…" Darlene counted. She was one of Larry's sisters, and she was "it." She was standing at the bottom of the hill with her arms crossed over her eyes, leaning her head against the large birch. As she counted, four of us—Larry, Nancy—another of Larry's sisters—and Johnny Storke, who lived one house this side of Einer Swenson's, raced away from where she stood.

Larry's voice was slightly more than a whisper. "Quick, this way!" He was running directly away from Darlene's backside heading for the pussy-willow bush at the swamp's edge. I raced to keep up as we crossed the broad area of mowed grass.

We entered the swamp at a dead run, and after only a few yards, Larry pointed his arm as he charged through the high grass. "Right there." He pointed to a large clump of un-trampled swamp grass.

"Got it!" I dove headfirst into the clump.

One of the things that made Larry and me two of the very best hiders ever was our knowledge of "camouflage" methods not known to the average person. We learned about camouflage while reading a Blackhawk comic book. The Blackhawk team was behind enemy lines, and Stanislaus taught them to hide right under the Germans' noses.

After hitting the ground, I burrowed to my left toward the thickest part of my patch. I had developed a technique allowing me to become nearly invisible in only seconds. I positioned my arms over my head hands together like I was diving into the water. By lying on my stomach and raising my butt a little, I could dig into the soft earth with the toes of my tennis shoes and move under the clump. We always wore tennis shoes while in the swamp to keep from getting cuts from the sharp edges of the long grass.

Over my heavy breathing, I heard, "24, 25… here I come ready or not." Whew, just in time!

There was dead silence.

This was the time I liked best. I was now in super-expert hiding mode as I sensed Darlene coming my way. I heard the swish-swish of her movement through the long grass as she circled to my left, just the other side of the willow bush. I lay still hardly breathing.

The hollow was a peat bog formed over the centuries by decaying vegetation and saturated with water. As summer moved toward fall, the natural cycle dried the spongy soil, which enabled me to feel each step as she walked straight toward where I was hiding. She stopped within inches of my curled body. There was no movement for about two minutes. I pictured her steely eyes moving slowly over the landscape as she stood there. Finally, she walked in the direction that Larry ran.

Absolute silence.

"Hey, you're it!" The sound exploded from somewhere on my right.

She had done what very few had been able to do. She found someone in the swamp; this was a major coup.

I listened as Larry tried his best to disqualify the transfer of "itsdom."

"No fair. You must have looked." Darlene kept telling everyone in earshot that Larry was now "it."

I lay in silent awe of her ability to discover the hiding place of her famous brother. How had she done it? I wondered if she peeked. Even if she did peek, it would have been impossible for her to see where we were hiding. What special powers did she have? Maybe she was like Wonder Woman. My mind sorted through the possibilities.

The sun had dipped beyond the horizon about 15-minutes earlier, and darkness was beginning to creep into the hollow. From where I lay, I heard Larry's complaints and claims of cheating while he moved away from my hiding spot. I laughed to myself, knowing that Larry was the one that got tagged. Honor compelled him to search for someone instead of me because he picked the clump that I now hid in.

It took a little while before I realized there was silence from his direction, nothing.

I strained to hear any sound from Johnny or Nancy.

There was still nothing.

Wait, what was that?

I heard a faint sound that seemed to be coming from behind me, the opposite direction from where Darlene tagged Larry. It sounded like it was far away; then, once again, nothing.

I lay there without moving for what seemed a very long time. Looking through the grass from my hiding spot beneath the clump, I saw the hollow was dark.

There was that sound again. It sounded a little closer, but still a long way off. What was it?

The only thing that kept me from jumping up and running as fast as I could was the fact that my friends were nearby—*Or were they?*

Say—It was starting to get creepy.

I tried to raise my head to look around only to find resistance from the swamp grass covering my head. And there was that sound again. It almost sounded like someone dragging something through the thick dry grass.

I had to see where the others were.

With a huge effort, I forced my body to rise through the grass to expose my head to the night air. I looked from side to side—nothing.

There was that noise again!

With my head above the swamp grass, it sounded different. It seemed like it was right next to me. What could be making that sound?

I propped myself on one elbow. The desire to avoid being found was beginning to be replaced by the desire to be safe on the front porch. There was no one else in the hollow. I was alone!

There's that dragging sound again.

What the heck? It was directly to my left. I stared in the direction of the sound. It felt as though my eyes were as big as my whole face. I moved my weight from my elbow to my hand so I could lift myself a little higher out of the grass. I felt goosebumps and a deep chill in the pit of my stomach.

At the exact instant that my hand touched the ground, and I began to lift myself for a better look, a new and powerful sound erupted.

"Screech—screech." An owl—a really loud owl—let out a scream that came from everywhere at once. I pictured him in the willow bush a little way in front of me, and I was positive he was going to swoop down and pluck my eyes from their sockets. Still, I was unable to move, frozen in place, afraid that if I moved, I would draw the attention of every animal in the swamp.

As the seconds passed, my heart returned to my chest, and the goosebumps began to subside.

Until—

The dragging sound came at the same time I felt something touch my hand. My eyes, now bugged out of their sockets, were focused on the weeds where I thought the sound originated. When I felt the touch, I looked at my hand just under the swamp grass.

A snake!

A big green snake with black and yellow stripes! Large round black eyes stared at me while a split tongue, black as night, flicked left and right.

My heart, for the second time that night, flew into my throat. It was more than I could stand, and I went from paralysis to warp speed.

I struggled to free myself from my hiding spot, every muscle pushing me through the grass that wanted to hold me there.

"Iiiieeeeeeeeeeee" was all that came out, and it was loud. I sprang up, feet already beating a speedy retreat toward the mowed grass. I cleared the swamp in about three jumps and raced toward the top of the hill, in the direction of our driveway, all the time screaming at the top of my lungs.

I was alone. My friends had gone to their own houses and the safety of a lit room.

The hill had grown slippery with the evening dew, and my well-worn tennis shoes couldn't grip the wet grass. Down I went. Scrambled to my feet; down again. It seemed the harder I tried to run up the steep hill, the less progress I made.

My breath came in gasps—any moment I expected to be devoured by some hideous swamp creature. I was glad there was no one there to see, yet I would have traded anything I owned for another person to share my fear. I was desperate as I reached down and with a single movement, pulled the shoes off my feet. I had to get better traction. I could imagine every creature in the swamp racing up the hill to where I sat. My screams, which stopped when I took the first fall, returned stronger than ever.

My bare feet, used to walking on all types of terrain, found sure footing as I continued my sprint toward the driveway and safety. When I came over the top of the hill and placed my first foot on the level ground, I sensed something to my left. It reached out and locked on my upper arm.

"Noooooooooo." I knew I was about to die.

"Dale. Dale, it's me, it's okay. It's me—Dad!"

I quit struggling. If it weren't for his firm grip, I would have collapsed on the spot. My breath came in fits and stops, never deep enough to fill my lungs.

"What in the world is going on?"

I heard him, yet he seemed to be miles away. I saw the lights from inside the house—behind the screens of my beloved porch. I saw the slope of the roof overhanging the front of the porch. I saw the stars in the dark sky above. And that's the last I remember of being outside in the driveway.

I still don't know how long I was out, but when I woke up, I was lying on the couch, my head in my mother's lap. She was stroking my forehead with a damp cloth, and my father sat on one of the dining room chairs brought in from the porch, his knees contacting the couch where I was lying. He was leaning toward me, elbows on his knees, face serious.

"You're okay, Dale. Dad carried you from the driveway. You're okay. You're safe here with us." My mother understood my confusion.

I was safe, what a wonderful feeling. They asked questions, and I explained the evening. They understood why I was afraid.

The three of us had milk and soda crackers, and I listened to my Dad talk about his horseshoe game, and my Mom telling him about the fire department auxiliary bake sale coming up. Things returned to normal.

Usually, it was my mother who tucked me in when I went to bed. Tonight my dad did the honors. I knew that whenever he was around, I would be safe.

We continued our evening games throughout the summer, but that was the last time I was caught alone in the swamp after dark.

CHAPTER 8

Turnquist's Woods

The sun was just beginning to peek through the thick trees as the 10-year-old hustled up the hill. His name was Larry Bursch, and when he stood very straight, he measured 47 inches on his Dad's tape.

Larry's dad, Harvey, was in the war. He came home a triumphant hero, met a beauty, married her, and moved to Fort Wayne, Indiana. He worked as a long-haul bus driver and began to build a family. He took a transfer in 1950 and moved his family of six to the island. Larry was the fifth child. Betsy-Leroy-Ronnie-Darlene-Larry-Nancy. Susan was born in 1953.

Nellie Bursch was a woman with natural grace and elegance, and she adored Harvey. They were poor by monetary standards, but very rich in family love and caring.

Harvey worked day and night to provide for his large family, and Nellie made the best of every situation that presented itself. Always impeccably dressed, she could be seen in the early morning pulling a bucket from the cistern that doubled as the refrigerator in the summertime, retrieving the bottle of milk so the kids could eat cereal for breakfast. Circumstance dictated near Stalinist tendencies when dealing with the kids. They were typical children, full of mischief and deviltry, but they were kept in line by her firm hand and no-nonsense manner.

Larry and I had a wonderful and free-flowing exchange of ideas, each respecting the other's viewpoint. He was a below-average student, but an above-average playmate. It wasn't so much that Larry couldn't learn what they taught in school, but a matter of perceived need; he failed to see the value of learning what they presented. He already knew how to read and write, so why study English? He could add and subtract, which was fine for him, figuring there would never be a need for long division or work with fractions or percents. No, he already knew enough to be a secure adult, although he never analyzed it further than tomorrow.

Larry wasn't always up this early, but when there was a plan in place, his excitement could hardly be contained, and this day, there was a plan. Not a concrete plan, more like an idea, but it was enough to get his juices flowing. It was early July, and he was headed to my house at the top of the hill. We were taking grandpa's flat-bottom boat to Pelican Island. The road on which he walked was little more than packed gravel, and at the top of the hill, its builders cut the roadbed into the terrain leaving jagged scars on both sides.

The East Wing of the porch became my bedroom during the summer. My feet were toward the rising sun, and the head of the bed was against the inside wall.

Larry walked to the screen and on tiptoes peeked inside the porch. "Psst, c'mon Dale. It's time to get goin'."

Mike's head shot up, his ears perked. Since we got him, he shared the bed with me. He was a mix: English Pointer and English Setter with long hair from the setter side. I remember when my sister brought him home. Just a puppy, he was white with black splotches on his back and shoulders, black ears, and small black pepper marks on his nose, face, and legs. He was now full-grown, always hungry, and invariably by my side.

My eyes popped open to sunshine bursts dancing on the screens. Although early in the day, it was already warm, and the Redwing Blackbirds trilled their morning songs from the swamp bushes behind the house.

Mike beat me to the floor as we jumped out of bed. I pulled jeans on over my swimsuit and headed for the front yard. No shoes, no shirt.

Careful not to let the screen door slam and wake up Mom and Dad, Mike and I met Larry in the front yard as he came around the side of the house.

"Ready?"

"Yeah, let's get goin'."

We broke for the road with Mike loping ahead. We sprinted across the yard, jumped over the hedge, and raced to the crest of the hill slapping the mailbox on the way. Mike was already there, tongue hanging out, ears perked, tail moving his whole butt from side to side, a look of pure pleasure on his face.

I casually asked the question. "Think we'll have any trouble gettin' the boat out?"

"Nah, no problem. What about the oars?"

"Gramps jams them under the seat before he turns the boat over. Should be there."

Larry and I walked in silence most of the way to Avalon. From a distance, we were identical, not yet at the gangly stage, although skinny with shoulder bones protruding and ribs prominent, he with brown hair, me with blonde bleached white by the sun.

Avalon was a lakeshore park. My parents were members of the Avalon Improvement Association and had the right to use the grounds. Huge trees grew on a flat grassy approach to the lake, and a cool breeze carrying the unmistakable lake smell made it one of our favorite places to picnic during the humidity of a Minnesota summer. Often, Dad played horseshoe with the other men at the pits that they built on one side of the property. Their talk was of jobs, the weather, and the chances of Eisenhower running for President. The women sat at a homemade picnic table provided by the Case family and talked about the kids, the dogs, and the neighbors not present.

I felt the gravel under my bare feet as we walked along the edge of the road, and I looked forward to taking the boat out. As my mind wandered, it came to rest on a piece of property that we needed to get to know better.

"Suppose we can explore Turnquist's woods?"

Larry looked at me with a sideways glance. Turnquist owned Pelican Point. None of us knew what Turnquist did for his money, and we'd never gone into Turnquist's woods. It's not that he ever did anything to us; in fact, I only saw him once. Donnie and I were walking on the road as he pulled into his long curving driveway. The windows on his black Cadillac were darkly tinted, but on this day, the driver's side was down. As he entered the mouth of the driveway and turned to look at us, his eyes seemed to cut to the center of my being. He was even bigger than grandpa's friend Einer Swenson. Einer was from the old country, stood over six feet tall, and asserted his thoughts with a strong accent, which made him in my mind, bigger than life. We decided it was best to cut Turnquist a wide berth.

Like the man, Turnquist's house was huge, and you couldn't see it from the road, but it sat on some of the nicest property on the island. Mostly, because of his apparent wealth and large house, Turnquist was a legend of sorts to my circle of friends and me.

I saw Larry's face brighten as he thought of the prospects of exploring those woods. They represented the one area on the island that was still a mystery to us.

"I hear he's got an icehouse up there. Sawdust and huge chunks of ice."

"Where'd you hear that?"

"Ronnie told me. I guess he's explored the woods." As he talked, Larry reached down, grabbed a stone, and tossed it at a stump.

"No kiddin'? Him and Doug?" My respect for Ronnie just went up. I grabbed a rock and aimed it at the same stump.

"Nah, just Ronnie. He told me he goes in there quite a bit."

I suspected Ronnie was a liar. He didn't appear to be the hero type. "No way. He ain't got the guts to do that alone."

We dropped the subject of Ronnie and the icehouse as we got close to the park.

We entered Avalon through the open gate on the right side of the parking area. Straight out from the dock is Wild Goose Island. Immediately to the left of Avalon, and about the same distance as to Goose Island, is Pelican Point. Once connected to Pelican Island, a narrow channel had been dug to allow boats to pass into the sheltered cove without entering the open bay.

Pelican Island was our original destination until we got to talking about Turnquist's woods. On one hand, row to a small island, hmmm—on the other, a military operation to skulk through enemy territory and explore uncharted ground. No contest. Grandpa's boat would have to wait for another day.

A brief strategy session on the dock at Avalon and we decided to enter the woods from Pelican Point itself. That meant exploring the shoreline all the way to the point before heading inland.

We planned to approach the big house from the lake side, circle to the left in the safety of the dense growth of trees, and work our way out to the perimeter road. From there, we had a wide choice of ways to go back home.

We always took turns being the leader, and this time Larry was in command during the first part of our foray.

We planned that Larry would take us to Pelican Point, a hard assignment because there were lots of places that were perfect for an ambush. Once at the Point, I would take command for the scouting mission around the main house. When we reached the perimeter road, we would be of equal rank once again, and if we were being chased, we would split up and meet back at the screen porch.

Larry was a very strict commander. He was an expert at hand signals and expected his men to understand and show blind obedience. There could be no talking, to risk giving away our position to the enemy.

We had gone maybe 100 yards when it became apparent that we had a serious problem.

Mike.

Not used to obeying hand signals, Mike surged ahead, splashing through the water around fallen logs, or chasing chipmunks from one fallen tree to the next. He regularly turned in my direction to see if I was still there, but try as I might to send necessary hand signals he went on his merry way.

Larry gave the sign for assembly.

I approached quietly and squatted by his side.

"What can we do with Mike?" His voice was a whisper.

This had been a problem before, and after much consideration, I came up with a surefire scheme for the next time it happened. Now was a good time to try it out.

"He's your advance scout." I hoped the commander would buy into it. Jeez, Larry was tough.

He pondered that thought. "Well, how in the heck can you keep him close? You gotta control the advanced scout, ya know."

The last time we patrolled a wooded area closer to home, I got court-martialed for not controlling Mike. *How could I control him when he didn't know the hand signals?* The commander set aside the court-martial— very strict, but forgiving.

"How about you signal me when he gets too far ahead? I'll whistle and bring him in."

Ever since Mike was a puppy, I whistled for him. He was accustomed to responding to a loud whistle, and I could let out a beauty. He never failed to race to my side, and besides—the enemy could easily mistake the whistle for a bird.

Larry bought.

The commander tested me mightily for the next 100 yards or so, and Mike responded like he knew the importance. All was well.

We were almost to Pelican Point and sensing the completion of his assignment, Larry intended to make the most of the last part of his command.

He signaled for assembly.

"There's booby traps just ahead. The only way to make our objective is to take the deadfall over the water."

Man, this was great. Larry was the greatest, most inventive commander ever.

"You got it, Commander. Lead the way.'"

And lead he did.

Larry scrambled along that fallen log just like a squirrel. The one time he almost fell, he recovered beautifully, yanking his foot out of the water to balance on the rough bark. Reaching the end, he launched himself the three feet or so, landing safely on shore well away from any booby-traps. He scanned for the enemy and, noting all clear, signaled for me to follow.

I was ready. I approached the stump end of the log and wound my way through the upturned roots, occasionally stopping to scan the immediate area for the enemy. Funny that Larry didn't go through the roots. My way was much more realistic.

Mud—created when my hands and feet, wet from wading in the water, contacted the exposed dirt within the root structure. By the time I crawled through the roots, my naked torso was streaked with thick black mud. Jeez, this was really neat. I scampered onto the trunk toward the far end where the commander waited, my bare feet in sure contact with the rough bark of the downed tree.

I stopped mid-stride, scanned the area for snipers—another two steps—stop—scan—another two steps.

That's when disaster struck.

My left foot, still holding goo from my trip through the roots, came in contact with the water left in the bark from Larry's near fall. Ordinarily, this would have been no problem. However, at that instant, I was in the process of reaching for the next handhold on the extended branches. As my foot slipped, my arms flailed, and I hit the water flat on my back.

Larry and I were both experts at improvising, especially in combat and patrol situations. I surfaced.

"I'm hit! I don't think I can make it to shore."

I knew I had him. Larry was about to join me in the water.

"Where are you hit, soldier?"

Quick—Think—Leg? I could limp with the best of them. Arm? To have a good arm wound, you needed a sling.

"Left leg!" My grimace would have made Gary Cooper proud.

"Here, grab this." He offered a dead branch. Jeez, this guy is good; he intends to stay dry.

"I'll try, sir," rolling on my right side. "I sprained my shoulder when I went down, but maybe I can hold it." Gotta get Larry in the water. "It's no use, sir. I can't hold it. I'm getting weaker. Don't know how much longer I can stay above water."

Larry's gonna get wet.

Larry's eyes began darting side to side "I think I hear an enemy patrol."

Sure enough, I heard it too. Something was coming our way. It sounded big. Bear? Nah. Wolf? Nah. Turnquist? Maybe. **MAYBE!**

It took me about two seconds to reach shore. By the time I got there, we both realized that we were being stalked. By Turnquist!

We lay on the shoreline in the shelter of fallen trees and waited for Turnquist to lose interest.

Crunch! Crunch! Stop—Silence—I could picture him. Not more than eight feet away, knowing we were here, yet not knowing *exactly* where. Tugging at his leather gloves—not work gloves like my father's, tight-fitting wrangler gloves like Buck Jones wears when he breaks broncos—he slowly surveyed the shoreline.

"Don't make a sound."

I didn't answer.

I could see Larry's forehead. He had a prominent vein that ran from his hairline down at a slight angle to his eyebrow. When we raced, the vein popped out. When we climbed trees, the vein popped out. As I now learned, when we were stressed, the vein REALLY popped out.

Neither of us dared to breathe. Turnquist was so close to us. Please don't let him step out to the shoreline. Please. Oh, why didn't we just take the flat bottom? Oh, please. Oh, please let us escape.

CRASH! The sound was deafening because it was so close. CRASH! The tall grass and small bushes that we hid behind began to stir. The dead tree that went directly over our position started to quiver, as though someone was walking along the trunk.

We're dead.

All at once, there was an explosion of activity. It was obvious that he intended to kill us for trespassing on his land. We heard him lurch in our direction. We heard him slash through the bushes. And we knew we were goners.

I looked at Larry's face. His vein was larger than I had ever seen it, and his eyes; his eyes were huge. How could a person's eyes swell that big without popping out of his head? He lay on his back; legs stretched toward the water, arms spread downward on each side of his body. It even looked like there was a trickle of spit forming at the corner of his mouth.

The grass parted, and a huge body flew between us landing on the shore inches from the water.

My mouth was opening and closing, but no sound came. Larry, on the other hand, was making the most terrifying sound I ever heard. With a voice that was loud, terror-stricken, and strangely death-defying yet totally submissive, Larry screamed.

"CRAPAHMAAAMAAA!"

What it meant we'd never know. Larry doesn't remember the word and swears he never said it. But he did.

Turnquist landed at the edge of the lake, spun around, and stared at us. His tongue was hanging out of the side of his mouth, and he was panting. He had a smile that extended from ear to ear. His ears were perked, and his head angled slightly to the side.

"MIKE!"

"Arrrrgggggg." Said Larry. "Stupid dog! Dumb mutt! Idiot dog! Jerk!" voice rising with every word.

Mike, tail wagging, sat his butt in the water and looked at us with his happy face as if to say, "Hi, guys."

I forgot my wounded leg. I was getting a little hungry. Maybe it's time to go home for lunch. Maybe we should finish scouting Turnquist's woods another day. Maybe we should head for home. Don't want to get in trouble for missing lunch.

CHAPTER 9

The Wednesday Night Fights

I n October 1950, I turned eight and was finding my niche in the neighborhood. I was a pretty gregarious fellow and made friends easily. Of course, those were the times that neighboring ladies welcomed new mothers with "a coffee," and the men with an invite for the new dad to a game of horseshoe. Times were slower and friendships more widespread. While my early friends lived along our road, Dad's were spread across a much wider area.

The carpentry additions to the house were completed, so Dad's evenings and weekends were no longer reserved for building projects. Still, home maintenance was ongoing, albeit in a much more relaxed manner, which gave him more time to enjoy his friends and family. He was making a good wage working at Strutwear Knitting, and life was good on the island.

* * *

I was excited. It was August 14, and it was Mom's birthday. That meant cake and ice cream. Only a special occasion warranted cake and ice cream. This year I would give her a present that would go down in history as one of the best gifts ever.

It's no secret that I loved cowboy comic books, and I knew Mom did too. One of my recent favorites was "Little Beaver," *Red Ryder's* young "partner," and I felt pretty strongly that Mom liked him almost as much as I did. With that thought in mind, I decided on her gift. At eight years of age, I had a clear idea of the value of art, and the masterpiece I would create would hold its own against the best the world had to offer.

I worked on it for hours, a reproduction by my own hand: a picture of Little Beaver's pony rearing on hind legs, mane flowing, forelegs extended, and tail wrapping magnificently around his hindquarters. It wasn't easy; draw, erase and redraw until it was perfect. Honestly, this was art worthy of framing.

I could hardly contain myself through dinner and thought I would explode with excitement until finally—"Happy Birthday To You."

Mom sat in her chair as Dad put the presents in front of her. Grandma Swanson sat to Mom's left.

I inched closer to the table, hoping she would pick my present first.

Wouldn't you know it; she picked Jill's and began to unwrap it. Oh, well, as they say, "save the best for last."

She held my sister's present, untied the string around the cardboard, and opened the flap. I watched, hypnotized, as first one glass slipper, then another was taken from the small box.

Oh, my gosh, salt and peppershakers. Jill had gone way overboard. She had spent her babysitting money and bought a gift like none other.

"Oh, thank you, honey."

Jill moved forward to receive a kiss from Mom. I swear I saw a smirk on her face as our eyeballs met.

"I'll bet there isn't another family on the island with such beautiful salt and pepper shakers. Oh, thank you. They're beautiful."

Okay—Okay. I was growing impatient.

Finally, she reached for my exquisitely wrapped, perfectly flat, bowless gift. The only wrapping paper I could find had pictures of Christmas tree ornaments and Santa's sleigh. Not exactly perfect for an August birthday, but I had cut it and carefully folded the edges to avoid damage to the artwork within. A couple of pieces of Dad's friction tape and it was ready for delivery.

I scanned the room; Dad was looking at Mom, and Jill was concentrating on something other than the moment at hand. The only one that seemed at all interested in my present was Grandma Swanson. It may have been because I talked it over with her when she let me use her bedroom to create it, and she was the only one who knew of my effort to make it perfect. Her eyes smiled as she watched Mom reach for the gift.

As Mom picked it up, she glanced at me with a conspiratorial glint in her eye, lifted the tape, and uncovered the masterpiece.

"What a wonderful drawing. Dale, you drew this just for me?"

"Yeah, Mom. It's Little Beaver's pony. Ain't he neat? Look at his mane and tail. I took special time on the mane and tail."

What she saw was a four-legged animal that resembled a rat standing on his rear legs, forelocks springing out between pointed ears, followed by dry-looking grass sticking in all directions, meant to be the flowing mane. At the back end of the animal, what looked like a scarf exited the body and wrapped around the nearest leg, tattered end flayed in all directions.

"Oh, Dale. It's wonderful. Al, would you look at what the kids gave me. I'm the luckiest woman alive."

With that, she got up and went into the kitchen with her new treasures.

"This is a perfect place for the salt and pepper shakers." She placed them on the stove between the two rear burners.

"And this is where the beautiful picture will go." She held it on the front door of the refrigerator, reached into the junk drawer, and came out with two Scotty dog magnets. One on each top corner and the gift was on display. I puffed up like a blowfish.

"You know, I think there is still one present left." Dad's voice drifted from the other room.

I shared a look with Mom, wheeled, and charged into the dining room to see what remained. There on the table was a small envelope. I looked for more, but there was nothing except the envelope.

Mom picked it up and pried it open with her long fingernails. Inside was a card; she just stood there, mute, gazing at it. I edged nearer, trying to see what it said.

All I could see was, "Love, Al.'"

That was it? That was Dad's gift? A card that said, "Love Al?"

Mom put the card on the table, walked to where Dad sat, pulled his head to her bosom, and gently kissed his forehead.

Then I noticed something else inside the card. It was a picture; cut from a catalog, and below the image was the word, Emerson.

* * *

I was beside myself when, a few days later, a truck pulled into the drive-way, and two men brought the most magnificent of electronic marvels into my life.

It was the latest invention, and it was called television. Word spread like wildfire. Soon neighbors were coming to the house to see this wonder mounted in a beautiful wood cabinet with speakers on both sides of the twelve-inch screen. Adding to the marvel was a record player in a drawer that pulled out from underneath the television. This record player, unbelievably, allowed records to be stacked on a shaft that held them above the turntable, automatically dropping the next record when the prior one finished playing.

Every Monday night, Mom lined up the dining room chairs, and the neighborhood kids watched *The Lone Ranger*. She seemed to enjoy hearing our comments and cheers as our hero swung into the saddle, waved his arm toward Tonto, and yelled "Hi-Yoooooo Silver, Haawaaaaaaaay.'"

Wednesday nights were reserved for the "Pabst Blue Ribbon Wednesday Night Fights," and Dad invited a few of the neighbors to join him. The regulars numbered five: Orville Neal, who lived one house this side of Turnquist; Einer Swenson, my grandpa's friend who lived at the end of our road; Harvey Bursch, Larry's dad, who lived just down the hill; and my Grandpa Johnson, who was on the island for his summer vacation. Of the group, Einer and Orville were the wild cards, often shadow boxing as though for the championship.

Well—One night, Orville made a big mistake that put an end to Dad's friends coming to watch the fights at our house.

On the night it happened, the men were in great spirits. They were on the front porch, talking about how their day went. I could hear them through the open door, and it sounded like Orville had a beauty. I heard him say he had to "straighten out his boss's way of thinking." According to Orville, nobody knows how to polish a car better than he, and his boss tried to tell him always to start polishing the bumpers first. Orville was quick to point out the "various factors that I use to determine the best place to start," and they were never the same from car to car. He was in the middle of what looked to be a long list of those factors when he was interrupted.

"It's almost nine." My mother spoke from the couch in the living room. She was knitting a scarf, or afghan, or something. She could transform a skein of yarn into the most amazing things. As a product of the great depression, she learned how to stretch a dollar and could knit and crochet anything you could buy off the shelf.

I was sitting in the hallway sorting through my comic book collection.

I heard Orville stop in mid-sentence, then the chairs scraping linoleum as the men pushed themselves away from the porch table. As they filed in, I could see the excitement on their faces. It looked like the night's fight was of more than average importance. Dad told Mom that one of the fighters, the name escapes me so I'll call him Moe Johnson, was from Minneapolis, and tonight's fight was his shot at the big-time.

I moved to where I could see the screen.

The men in the room were sitting in two rows. The front row, Orville, Einer, and Harvey, were seated in three straight-backed dining room chairs set about two feet apart on the large braided rug that covered the living room floor. Each had placed their coffee cups on the floor. The back row was the living room couch. Sitting at one end was my father, at the other, Grandpa Johnson. Each had a full cup of coffee; Dad's on the end table—Grandpa's on the floor between his feet.

It started in the first round. Toe to toe, they stood in the center of the ring trading punches. The only way I could tell them apart was by the color of their trunks: one black, one white.

Grandpa was the first to speak. "I'm betting on Schmidt."

"No way," replied Harvey, "Johnson will kill him."

I couldn't tell Johnson from Schmidt, but it looked like the guy in white was getting the best of the guy in black.

Grandpa quietly stated that Johnson didn't have a chance while my father joined him in favor of Schmidt. Einer was unsure but thought he favored "dat goldang Johnson, da up an' comer."

That left only Orville to declare, "I got fifty bucks that say Johnson knocks him out inside of ten."

Five heads snapped in Orville's direction, Einer's, Harvey's, Grandpa's, my father's—and my mother's. Never before had anyone bet money on the outcome of a boxing match. The room was as quiet as a tomb. I watched Dad and his friends as they looked at each other, obviously eager to meet the challenge. Just as my father started to open his mouth, a soft but firm, "Allen," came from Mom. Dad, mouth formed to speak, turned in her direction, and immediately changed his mind about taking Orville's bet.

I have never heard a single word that could change the way things happened like that word could. It seemed that "Allen" was used only when Mom wanted to make a point. It wasn't just the word exactly. It was the delivery.

Nobody said anything for about a minute when all of a sudden, the silence was broken by the crowd noise from the television. I didn't see him go down, but Johnson was flat on his rump in the middle of the ring.

"Get up! Get up!" Orville shouted as he jumped from his chair. Johnson continued to sit on the canvas, arms out to his sides, the backside of his gloves resting on the ring surface, chin propped on his massive chest. The referee pushed Schmidt toward one of the corners and returned to Johnson's side, where he started to swing his arm in time with his shouted count.

My mother's eyes were fixed squarely on the television.

"One. Two. Three. Four." Johnson sat there.

"Get up, you bum." Orville was now on his feet, arms gesturing wildly. Mom's eyes moved to Orville.

"Five. Six. Seven." The arm, swinging with the count, started above the ref's head and shot down as though throwing a rock into a pool with such force that I thought his hand would fall off.

"Aw, shoot," said Orville as he dropped his body toward the chair.

"Nine. Ten!" With the ten-count coming at the exact moment that Orville's butt hit the chair.

It was like slow motion. The chair started to twist sideways, and there was a crunching sound as the wood began to splinter.

Mom's eyes widened.

Orville's left leg stretched toward the ceiling as he tried to move his right foot to keep from falling. The move smashed the coffee cup sitting on the floor, splashing coffee over the braided rug.

Mom's mouth fell open.

Orville, body out of control, was heading right for Einer Swenson. Einer, seeing what was coming, reacted like a cat and dove to his right. The trouble was—his dive landed him squarely in Harvey's lap, and another cup broke; more coffee on Mom's rug. Worse yet, Harvey's chair, locked to the braided rug as though glued, broke into a million pieces, and both he and Einer landed on the floor right in front of Mom.

While all this was happening, Dad threw his arms out to avoid chair shrapnel, brushing his coffee cup off the end table and sending it against the wall.

Mom sat, slack-jawed, eyes like dinner plates, and surveyed the damage.

Orville was lying over Einer's empty chair. Next to him, lay Einer and Harvey piled on the sticks and broken wood that used to be another chair. Right behind Orville sat Dad, ashen-faced and mute. The only one unscathed was Grandpa, and I watched as he bent over, picked up his coffee cup, and leaned back on the couch looking in my mothers' direction.

I followed his eyes toward Mom, and it was apparent she was about to erupt. Her face was calm, but her eyes were on fire. She saw three broken coffee cups, coffee soaking into the rug, two chairs that were now kindling, a groaning Orville rubbing his ribs, two men in a heap on the living room floor, and a husband that was, for the moment, struck dumb.

Her eyes moved across the accident scene until they fixed on one of the smashed coffee cups, shards visible from beneath the crushed chair.

"Allen," she said, slightly louder than she had spoken the word earlier.

Dad's mouth snapped shut as he spun his head to look in her direction.

Orville seemed to be having trouble concentrating; his head turned from the television screen to my father, to my mother, and then back to the small screen, all the while his face projecting—"oh, oh, what do I do now?"

Grandpa just sat on the couch, sipping his coffee, eyes slanted in Mom's direction.

"Will you please pick up this mess while I get some towels," She was clearly furious and speaking in a barely audible voice.

The men, all except Grandpa, hurried to pick up the chair pieces and broken cups. Dad picked his cup up off the floor in the middle of the front porch, where it came to rest after glancing off the wall and careening through the open doorway from the living room miraculously intact but splattering coffee against the wall where long brown stains now worked their way toward the floor.

While all this was going on, Grandpa continued sipping his coffee, not saying a word.

Not wanting any part of what was happening, I lit out for the hallway just off the living room.

Mom came back with towels and told the men to roll the rug back exposing the brown puddles on her beloved hardwood. She used the towels to dry the area then had the men spread the wet part of the rug over itself to dry. Dad's friends complied with every wish, but as soon as they were done, they were out the door.

"So long, Al."

"See ya, Al."

"See ya tomorrow."

Even Grandpa. "Thanks for the lovely evening."

Dad stood, stooped shoulders, to face the music alone.

"I don't think it's a good idea to have the guys over for the fights, do you, Al?"

I never heard his answer, but from then on, Dad and I watched the Wednesday Night Fights without the neighbors.

I remember some of the fighters like Sugar Ray Robinson and Carmen Basillio. I wonder what happened to the fighter I called Moe Johnson.

CHAPTER 10

The Drowning

A s happens in small communities all across America, Island Park residents determined that a community service, one designed to protect the wellbeing of the residents, was needed. Shortly after we moved there, and after considerable debate, it was decided that a fire department would help bring the community into the modern world.

Strangely, the decision was not the result of a tragedy. It was simply due to the good sense of the people living there.

With his house across the road from the village hall, where department meetings could be held, the obvious choice for Fire Chief was Al Boll, our resident entrepreneur. He already had the summer ice concession, which was becoming less and less a necessity, and he owned the required garage space for the island's road maintenance vehicles, with enough room for a temporary home for the fire equipment until a garage could be added to the village hall. In addition to that, his house's location near the island's center, at the convergence of access roads, was well-positioned for responding to residents' needs regardless of their location on the island. We had a Chief, and as today in many rural areas, volunteers were husbands, brothers, and fathers.

My Dad was a volunteer fireman.

There were two methods of notifying the firemen when a calamity occurred. Both were controlled from the chief's house.

The siren would sound, and the number of times it cycled indicated the type of emergency. As I recall, one extended blast indicated the meeting call, two blasts, a fire, and three blasts indicated a potential drowning.

The second method, which was used in conjunction with the siren, was a specially coded number of rings on the telephone. Ours, like all others on the island, was connected to several homes in a configuration known as a "party line." The number and duration of rings told you if the call was for your house, or for another's; one long ring, two long rings, two longs and a short, and so forth. People were on the honor system to respect the privacy of their neighbors (I suspect that many conversations of a private nature weren't very private at all).

Dad's status as a volunteer fireman meant I was one of the "informed few" that knew the meaning of the various signals. This was good for a feeling of importance, and I admit that I made the most of this privilege in seeking influence with my friends.

* * *

There were three stores on Island Park. Grimm's store was inland, Pembroke store was on the East Side of the island facing Spring Park Bay, and Hildebrandt's was overlooking Cook's Bay on the road to Enchanted Island. Of the three, Grimm's was our favorite.

Mr. Grimm was a soft-spoken man with the patience of an oak tree. He would allow us to hover over his fantastic collection of penny candy, while we tried to decide what we wanted for our money. This process could be excruciatingly slow, and I suspect it could also drive a storekeeper nuts. Mr. Grimm's kindly manner was enough to keep us coming back, but he had something else that ensured his number one status amongst my friends and me: He offered a two-scoop ice cream cone for a nickel! Nothing tasted better than one of his ice cream cones on a hot summer day, and we all considered Grimm's as the place to go when we had money in our pocket!

We were outside of Grimm's, Dickey, Larry, Ronnie, and I. Ronnie was the new kid, moving into a house near the village hall.

It was early afternoon, and it was one of those hot, hot days as is typical during Minnesota summers when the humidity hangs in the still air like a Finnish Sauna. You could see the heat rise from the packed gravel of the road, appearing as puddles of water shimmering in the distant depressions.

There was no conversation as each of us concentrated on licking the melting ice cream before it ran down the outside of the cone. Ronnie was losing the race. For some reason, he never thought to turn the cone and clean up the far side. He already had vanilla and chocolate running over his knuckles.

"Hey! Dummy!" It was Dickey. "You got ice cream all over your hand!"

"Aw, Jeez!" Ronnie spun his hand to get to the far side of the cone. The melting ice cream ran off his fingers like it was coming from a faucet. Shirt, pants, feet, his whole front side was splattered with it. I looked at Dickey. He just rolled his eyes, shook his head, and continued to tend to his own cone.

Ronnie was one of those kids that held remnants of his last meal around the edges of his mouth. It always seemed to accumulate at the corners. He also had a weakness for sinus infections, resulting in yellow snot that sometimes bubbled when he became excited. We got used to it, but it caused him quite a bit of grief.

Once you start to lose the battle with an ice cream cone, things tend to go bad in a hurry. Ronnie was a testament to that. By the time he finished, his legs were spread, body leaning forward, as melting ice cream puddled between his feet.

"Let's see if the Skelly station has any red rubber." Larry was finishing his cone, wiping his hands on his jeans.

The Skelly gas station had two pumps and a one-car garage that enclosed a deep pit used for oil changes and whatever else required access to the underside of a vehicle. A small doorway attached the garage area to a small office, which like the garage, opened to the gasoline pump. The building backed up to a ravine, which provided the station owner with a perfect place to throw his junk. The Skelly Station was where we went to look for old inner tubes. It was a bonanza for slingshot rubber, and it had been quite a while since we last searched.

The four of us shared looks.

"Great idea." I hopped from the wooden landing in front of the store onto the edge of the road. My friends did the same, and we moved in unison toward the station standing on the other side.

We all heard it at the same time. It started as a low growl, building in intensity and increasing in pitch until it became a scream. THE FIRE SIREN! We stopped in the middle of the road, turning in the direction of the sound. The scream held, subsided to a low growl, only to repeat itself building to a scream once again. Two blasts. Again, it softened, and again it repeated, building to a crescendo then again dying. Then nothing.

Three blasts! "A drowning!" All my senses came to life.

We moved as one, sprinting up the hill that ran in front of the station, cutting into the woods, and onto the shortcut that gave us the quickest route to the fire station.

"Watch the log!" Dickey vaulted a downed tree spanning the path through the woods.

I was second, and behind me raced Larry, followed in turn by Ronnie. I timed my leap perfectly, landing with one foot on top of the log, and vaulted over the dead branch protruding from the other side.

This made life worth living. The joy and freedom of running barefoot, full tilt, trees whipping past us, all our senses alive anticipating the next obstacle. We ran, brushing small branches away with our arms, feeling disdain at their feeble attempt to hamper our lightning fast progress. Adrenaline flowed (we were not yet familiar with testosterone).

That's when Ronnie approached the fallen tree.

All I heard was a muffled "Oufffff.'"

I stopped, causing Larry to crash into me, sending us both sprawling.

"What the heck did you stop for?"

We picked ourselves up off the ground.

"It sounded like you fell." I rubbed my elbow to ease the new hurt and looked toward the fallen tree where Ronnie was rolling side-to-side, groaning pitifully. "Oh, great! Ronnie's down." Dickey was quickly disappearing from view, intent on being the first one to the fire station.

"You alright?" I yelled in Ronnie's direction. No answer, just side-to-side moans.

As we understand as adults, priorities in a kid's mind are most often dictated by the circumstance at the time. On the one hand, we had a potential drowning; on the other, we had an injury to one of our comrades. I heard the sirens from the fire trucks as they raced from the garage. *Sorry, Ronnie!*

"We'll meet you at the station!" I yelled, breaking toward the sound. I was pretty sure that Ronnie's injury wasn't that serious.

We exited the woods on the edge of the hill behind the village hall, where the trees yielded to a sheer drop-off created when the land was excavated to make a flat spot for the building. Here at least, common sense prevailed, and we walked along the slope on the edge of the precipice, which eventually reached the same level as the station.

"It took you guys long enough." Dickey sauntered out of the open garage door. "The trucks already left."

"Ronnie fell when he tried to jump the tree."

"Is he alright?"

"I think so." Larry began explaining Ronnie's fall.

I was more interested in checking out the empty garage. I knew, from being with my Dad during earlier emergencies, that the chief would write the location of the current crisis on a blackboard at the back of the garage area. The chalkboard was to inform the other volunteers who arrived after the trucks left.

I darted through the open door and ran toward the back of the darkened building. My eyes, which were accustomed to the bright sunlight, made it appear as though I had just entered a cave. I focused on the small window that I knew was directly over the blackboard. It was like running in a tunnel, unable to see left or right.

"Come on!" I heard Larry's excited voice. "The trucks already left. You alright?"

It must be Ronnie, I thought. I guessed that nothing was broken.

As I ran toward the back wall, I heard the others charging in behind me. The blackboard beckoned. It appeared to be blank. My eyes were riveted to the black square, everything else a dark void. Another stride forward. Was there writing? YES! Two more giant strides brought me to the message board. My eyes were beginning to adjust. Something was written on it in light blue chalk, and it looked like it started with a "P." I edged closer.

P E M B R O K E—D R O W N I N G

I spun around, "Someone drowned at Pembroke!" The excitement caused my voice to be high-pitched and louder than necessary. Larry stopped at my side, while Dickey arrived seconds later.

"What'd you say?" Ronnie, coming at a dead run from outside the open door, cut into the garage much closer to the outer wall than where we entered moments earlier. He was about to receive his second injury of the day.

The firemen backed the trucks into the garage, and once, the result of inattentiveness or simple misjudgment, the driver hadn't stopped in time. The result was a crushed locker that stood against the back wall. To prevent a repeat of this horrible miscue, one of them thought of a method to signal the driver when to stop the truck. Their solution was to attach a hinged board to the sidewall that would line up with the driver's window when he had backed the proper distance. The board would be folded against the wall when the trucks were in the garage, allowing for free movement around the vehicle.

Unfortunately, the trucks were now out of the garage, and the board was extended.

Ronnie, as good as blind after going from bright sunlight into the darkened garage, was running with gusto. His mouth was opening, and we could hear a word just starting to form when his forehead made contact. We looked in horror as his feet kept running while the rest of his body seemed to lose momentum. A dull thwack was all we heard. His head and neck seemed to scrunch down into his shoulders as his arms flew forward. He seemed suspended in mid-air before he finally landed with a dull plop, squarely on his behind, directly underneath the vibrating board.

"Holy cow! You alright?" It was Dickey who was the first to reach him.

"Aaaaah…Oh, jeez." Ronnie was looking at us, but with a blank gaze. His feet were straight out in front of him as he sat on his butt, holding himself upright with both arms angled rearward, palms resting on the cement floor. "Oh, jeez, does that hurt." His forehead had a huge welt that ran from side to side where his hairline began. "Am I bleeding?"

"No, no blood." Dickey, the oldest, therefore the most experienced, took the leadership role. "Ronnie, you better lay down for a while. Here." Dickey offered his hands and cradled the injured head as Ronnie lay back. Larry and I looked on, mute, afraid, concerned, and yet I remember feeling a tinge of impatience. After all, we had a drowning to deal with.

A few minutes elapsed before Ronnie got to his feet. "Jeez, I almost killed myself." He looked terrible. "Boy, do I have a headache. I think I'll just go home."

We consoled him as best we could, commenting on his speed upon entering the garage, noting his athletic ability as he avoided smashing his head on the floor when he went down, and we marveled at his ability to take a blow. He left, sore and aching, but with his confidence buoyed. As he limped toward home, we again turned to the message on the blackboard.

After a brief consultation, we decided to go to our houses and get our bikes. From there, we could ride like the wind to the drowning at Pembroke.

* * *

We still think our mothers entered into a conspiracy, because one by one, as we came to our homes, they stood waiting at the door. Larry was first because his house was at the bottom of the hill.

"You better come in and eat."

"Can't come in now Mom, I need my bike. We're gonna ride to Pembroke."

"No, you're not!"

"Aw, Mom. Come on."

"Don't 'AW MOM' me, young man. Dinner will be ready in a little while. Say goodbye to Dale and Dickey. You're coming inside."

We shuffled our feet, looked at the ground, examined our hands, and did our best to look casual during the exchange. We heard Larry protesting as his mom hauled him in the front door, then we headed up the hill to find the same treatment, with minor variations, waiting for us when Dickey and I tried to get to our bicycles.

That evening was the longest of my life as I waited for Dad to come home. He wasn't there for dinner, and he still wasn't there when the sun set behind the trees to the West. As the hours passed, the more agitated my mother became when I tried to ask questions about the drowning, remaining steadfast in referring to it only as "The Fire Call."

"Dad's still at The Fire Call." Was about all I could get out of her.

Finally, she sent me to bed in the back bedroom with the promise to awaken me when Dad got home—no matter how late. I knew something was drastically wrong because she sent me to the back bedroom. I always slept on the porch during the summer, but I could see there would be no compromise, so I obediently retired.

What could possibly cause this sudden change in sleeping arrangements? My mind, full of excitement at the day's happenings, was now filled with questions.

I tossed and turned, unable to get to sleep, for what seemed like hours. Finally, I heard the crunch of gravel and saw the trees at the back of the house light up from the headlights on Dad's car. I jumped from bed and raced through the kitchen, through the dining room, and onto the front porch.

Mom and Dad were in the front yard. They were embracing, and I stood there respecting the scene and their private time. My mind was racing, but now, instead of excitement and unanswered questions, I was feeling fear. Fear of things not understood, caused by what I witnessed in the front yard where my parents still clung to one another.

Finally, my mother stepped back, took my Dad by the hand, and as they walked together up the steps and into the porch, their slumped shoulders and lowered heads sent a chill through my body.

Without looking in my direction, my mother quickly crossed the porch, entered the living room, and disappeared from sight, her feet padding softly as she crossed the braided rug, and then the wooden floor leading through the archway and down the short hall to their bedroom.

Dad looked in my direction. His eyes were red and his hands were trembling as they hung by his sides. Then he slowly raised his arms and extended them in my direction as he stepped to gather me. I rushed to him, closing my arms around his waist, feeling his strength around my shoulders. Then I started to sob, knowing that something terrible had happened.

I never wanted to let him go as we stood together on the front porch. The night sounds were crystalline, so loud and so friendly, my soft crying seeming to blend in perfect harmony with the chorus of frogs and crickets just outside the screens.

"There was a drowning today." His voice was soft as he slid onto a chair by the table. I could feel my breath catch in my throat as I tried my best to be a man. "It was Bobby Finch."

Involuntarily, my body began to shake as the tears began to stream down my face. Bobby was older than I was, but I knew him. My father gently lifted me to his lap, and I buried my face in his broad chest, feeling the harshness of his wool shirt, even as I felt the tenderness with which he held me.

"He was swimming off the raft at Pembroke. There were five boys, and they were horsing around pushing each other into the water, then climbing back on. They don't know what happened, but before they realized it, Bobby wasn't there."

Dad continued to explain, as best he could, about the tragedy that happened that day. As I sobbed, his words brought a strange comfort to me. His words, or the way he delivered them, with tenderness and care, made me realize the importance of life.

I felt the sadness of the story, but I had not yet realized the true sadness of the drowning being felt by all the families on the island. After a very long time, my father stood and carried me to the back bedroom and with great care, placed me on the bed and tucked the covers around my small shoulders. He stood and looked down at me, then bent, kissed my forehead, straightened and walked from the room.

As I lay there, I could hear my mother's soft crying through the wall.

I learned about pain that night. I learned about sorrow, and I learned of the closeness of the residents on the island. We were all family.

CHAPTER 11

The Rudder Debacle

When I was eleven, a year after my dad and Jim Wendt started the Boy Scout troop on the island; Jim moved his family to a house located across the street from Phelps Bay. The road had been upgraded from gravel to concrete. Narrow, by restricted space, it was the only such road on the entire island. Local residents referred to the stretch along the bay as the Gold Coast. Jim decided, since he was now living in a house with lake access, it was time to become a sailboat owner. Like a lot of people living on the island, he lacked the resources to purchase a sailboat. Unlike most of the people living on the island, he decided he would make his own.

His opening gamut was to purchase an old, twelve-foot rowboat from someone down the street, and with great care, Dad and Jim carried it to the basement door and eased it inside and onto the sawhorses that waited. Jim purchased plans for a sailboat from a magazine, and construction began. They followed the instructions to a "T", at least most of them, taking shortcuts only when they were positive their action would not deter from the operation of the finished craft.

Dad invited me along when they first started, but soon realized I was more trouble than a helper. When I was paying attention, it was one question after another, and when I lost interest, I became a pest, so he went without me.

They worked in the evenings, from early spring until sometime in July, before they declared the thing ready for the water. It was a Saturday, bright sunshine with a light wind when dad and I pulled into Jim's driveway.

"Ready to go?" Jim met us at the basement door.

"Let's see if this baby floats." Dad's proclamation struck me as a bit late in the process. After all, they had been working on the thing for several months, and I assumed it would float.

"Oh, she'll float alright. Let's drag her out to the pickup."

I followed them into the basement through the walk-in door at the edge of the driveway.

"What do you think?" Dad was justifiably proud of the finished product.

I was amazed at the transformation from a worn-out, decrepit rowboat, to the gleaming, streamlined, wonderfully painted thing of beauty in front of me. They had scraped and sanded the entire hull and painted it a shiny white that shone like a beacon in the confines of the basement. Running down each side, just above the waterline, was a bright red stripe. Sitting like it was, on the sawhorses, I couldn't see the top, but it was clear that changes had been made there as well. Circling to the back, I saw a rudder attached to the transom with a series of clamps encircling the main shaft. It was their genius that would allow the rudder assembly to be slid up and down to accommodate deep or shallow water.

It seemed that Jim took special pride in building the rudder itself, made from scratch with his own two hands, and consisting of a blade from a canoe paddle screwed firmly in place to the main shaft, itself the transformed body of one of the oars that came with the boat. The paddle blade was intended to be beneath the water when in operation and controlled by grasping the handle, now cut short and screwed to the top of the same oar body, at more or less right angles. The whole thing looked like a perverted letter Z.

Dad lifted me so I could see inside the boat. I was awestruck. They had added two decks, one at the very front, just under the gunwales.

The other was amidships, and overlapped the gunwales, like a cover on a box. In the center of this cover was a reinforced hole to accommodate the upright mast for the sail. On the inside bottom of the boat was a hollow block designed to hold the base of the vertical pole.

There was also a sail that looked an awful lot like a bedsheet, and some rope and a couple of pulleys linked to a half-inch galvanized pipe intended to be used somehow for raising and lowering the sail. "Wow! You guy's otta go into business building boats."

The two of them shared a look. "Yeah, sure—lots of money in that I'll bet."

Dad put me back on the floor, and they moved to either end of the beautiful new sailboat. As they lifted, I pulled the sawhorses to one side, and they headed for the door. That's when they ran into trouble.

It seems that with the new deck amidships, the darn thing got hung up on the doorframe. They backed, twisted, came at it from as many angles as space allowed, all to no avail.

Finally, faces red from exertion, they carefully set it down on the basement floor. "Dang. I measured. This should fit." Jim had a dejected look on his face.

"Well—let's try tipping it sideways and see if she'll go—No. Let's measure it and see if it'll fit before we try." Dad wasn't about to give up. Out came the tape measure.

"Seems like we had to tip it getting it in, didn't we, Al?"

"Doesn't make a difference, Jim. The new deck for the mast makes her too big for the opening, even if we do tip her."

"How about we try to get it angled corner to corner. Ya think it'll go then?"

A few measurements later..."Naw, that won't do it either."

They decided it was time for a beer.

Leaning against separate sawhorses, their morale in the toilet, they stared at the opening, clearly too small to accommodate the new boat. One by one, they would stand, circle the boat, move to the doorway, examine the opening, and return to the boat, reconsider the problem, and return to the sawhorses for another chug of beer.

"Dang—I sure don't want to take off the deck. We got that sucker screwed on and glued so tight we'd have to wreck it to get it off. How about we take the door off its hinges? That'd give us another inch or two."

"No, I thought of that. It still won't go." Dad got up to get a close look at the door. "You know what might work, though. How about we take off the door and remove the doorframe. That would give us another few inches. We can put her back in place. No damage done."

A few measurements later, and the plan was in place. Jim made Dad promise they would replace the door before launching the boat, which was readily agreed to, and within ten minutes, the vessel was in the back of the pickup. Another ten minutes and we were on our way.

Jim's house was the last on the road, with only a short trip to the end, where the terrain dropped to lake level. They unloaded the boat, pushed it into the water where dad stood, pants rolled above his knees, holding it in place until Jim drove the truck back to the house and rejoined us at the launch site. I was lifted into the bow, finding the small front deck a perfect place to sit, while dad and Jim climbed aboard, dad on the center deck and Jim at the tiller. They lifted the mast into place, raised the sail, and like mariners of old, we headed for the open water.

As we progressed further into the lake, the wind, which seemed light to moderate on the shore, was now brisk, and waves lapped on the sides, threatening to come over the top of the gunwales. Like a seasoned veteran, Jim maneuvered the craft, so we were pointed downwind, and we picked up speed. We were going so fast that I crawled off the deck, afraid that I might be thrown overboard. I looked at dad. His eyes were alight with excitement, his tan face, and short-cropped hair dripping with spray put up by the fast-moving boat.

"Whoo-ee. This baby is flying."

"Hold on—going to starboard." Jim perfected a turn toward the open lake as the sail swung to the left, barely missing dad as he dove to the bottom of the boat. From where I sat, I could see the top of his head, and as he turned to the front, his eyes no longer held the same excitement as was there earlier.

"Don't you think we should head closer to shore?"

"C'mon Al—this is livin."

"Turn it toward shore, Jim."

"Alright."

With near perfect precision, he leaned on the tiller, and the boat came around, heading toward the shore. Dad tugged on the rope attached to the sail beam, and it swung over his head to catch the wind from the other side. We were now moving at an alarming clip directly toward shore and the docks that stretched into the water. The sail, small by design, caught the wind, and the boat tipped perilously close to capsizing.

The calm look on Jim's face turned to one of alarm as he pushed the tiller to bring us into the wind. There was a loud crack as the paddle separated from the shaft, and the look on Jim's face became one of alarm, as he almost fell over the side. We were now rudderless.

"Al, take the sail down. Quick."

Dad jumped into action, nearly tipping us over, as he reached to release the rope holding the sail aloft. Our progress slowed, and in a short time, we were drifting with the waves. Whether by design or through blind luck, the single oar remaining from the original rowboat was jammed under the center deck. As I cowered in the front of the boat, Jim and dad took turns paddling us into one of the docks.

The maiden run was over. Jim's handmade rudder was broken, the bottom half missing, his ribs were sore from smacking the gunwale, and his spirit was shattered. I looked toward dad, now sitting on the edge of the dock, feet in the boat. The alarm on his face while in the heat of action was now replaced with an impish grin, eyes aglow with humor... and he began to laugh.

CHAPTER 12

World Record Racer

We moved with purpose as we trudged up the steep hill alongside Ronnie's house. Intended as a permanent road in the future, it was now nothing more than a gravel track, bone dry from the summer heat, and dusty from lack of fall rains. The grass, growing in sparse tufts on its surface, was brown and brittle. We were about to make our high-speed run.

The prior Christmas, I had received a book titled, *"Boys Fun Book—things to make and do"* from my Aunt Margaret. It was loaded with ideas. Some were science-based and easily completed, some were clearly above the abilities of a ten-year-old, and more than a few would be a challenge for me today. One of them, however, popped into my mind during one of our dump-picking sessions when we found an old wagon that someone had thrown out. The *Boys Fun Book* showed a soapbox derby racer with a kid in the cockpit and included plans for building the thing right down to the axles and wheels.

That was the start of our next project and is what brought us to Ronnie's hill.

"Man-o-man, this is gonna be sumthin'! Johnny single-handedly pulled our contraption to the top, and we now positioned it facing downward.

There were just four of us: Johnny, Larry, Ronnie, and me.

It took us a few hours to build, and it was the finest cart ever constructed. While a trained engineer would have made safety a priority, we weren't trained engineers. While skilled production line workers would have made sure everything fit to a "T." We weren't them either. The result was a hodge-podge of wood, wheels, and connecting hardware, which, under close examination, would have revealed itself as death on wheels.

After we all had a turn in the cockpit on the hill in front of my house, we decided we needed something a little more challenging. We were now poised at the top of one of the steepest hills on the island.

"How fast do you think it'll go? Larry was anxious.

"I'll bet it goes like sixty." Johnny was firmly planted in front of our masterpiece to keep it in place.

"You kiddin' me? Nothin' can go that fast—especially nothin' we built. Ronnie had a big glob of snot in his right nostril, remnants of his latest sinus infection.

My enthusiasm was waning as I looked down the uneven surface. I was the big shot that said I'd drive. No problem, I said. No big deal, I said. The longer I stood there, the bigger deal it became.

My parents bought me a winter cap last year, leather, with flaps over my ears tipped with strings that tied under my chin. I figured it would make a great safety helmet, and I now pulled it from the rear pocket of my jeans.

"You bring the tape"?

"Yep, got it right here. Larry was fiddling in his shirt pocket, digging for the roll of Dad's friction tape I brought from home. After retrieval, he began wrapping it around my elbows. We figured it would offer a little protection in case something happened, like a crash or something. On the way up the hill, Ronnie went into his house and came out with a couple of his little sister's doll pillows that Larry taped on the outside of each elbow.

"All set. Climb aboard, Captain, and let's see what this baby can do."

For some reason, I didn't feel well as I climbed into the cockpit, an orange-crate with the divider ripped out. We nailed the crate to a long plank that served as the frame, carefully selected from Dad's stock because of the hole near the end. It wasn't very stable since the orange crate was about three times wider than the board, but it worked in the trial runs, so that wasn't an issue.

We used the axles and wheels from the wagon, held in place with bent nails. Our front axle board had a hole in it, a little off-center, but close enough to the middle for us to bolt the thing together. The single bolt allowed the front to turn, and was steered with twine reins tied just inside each front wheel. It was a little tricky to drive at first, but I proved to be a master at steering during the trial run.

"You ready?"

I changed my mind. No way was I going down this hill. Now or ever.

I moved to get out, and Johnny, bracing the cart, took it as a signal to let 'er go.

Oh, my gosh! I was moving—down the steepest hill on the island.

All I wanted to do was get out of that cockpit. Holy cow! Too fast, too fast.

I grabbed hold of the reins, elbows banging the sides of the orange-crate, and settled in, determined to reach the bottom in one piece. I began talking to God, "Now I lay me down to sleep"—The only prayer I knew.

I was going faster than ever before, even on my bike, and my eyes were bouncing around in their sockets so much I couldn't focus. Gravel spit from beneath the uneven wheels, and I gained speed with every yard.

The gang tried to keep up with me at the beginning, but now they stood watching my run, mostly hidden by the dust cloud surrounding me.

"Look at that sucker go. Larry was ecstatic. "Man, he's goin' at least sixty!"

I later figured I was about halfway down when the nails on the right side of the axle gave way, and I saw the flayed end of a twine rein fly past my face. The cart took a right-angle turn, and I felt myself airborne.

I can't say my life flashed in front of me, but I knew I was dead.

It felt like I was in the air for a long, long time before I hit the gravel and skidded to a stop. I don't remember much about the landing, but by the time my senses returned, Larry was charging toward me.

"You all right? Man, you must'a been goin' a hundred!"

Ronnie slid to a stop a few feet away. "Holy crap, were you flyin'. Holy crap, you must'a been doin' two hundred!! You okay?" He now sported a yellow bubble from his nose.

One thing Ronnie brought to the gang was some colorful phrases we never heard before. Larry and I were raised Lutherans, and Johnny was a Catholic. Ronnie was brought up…umm…in Cleveland. We never thought to ask what religion he was, but he brought us more than a few new sayings when he moved in.

Somehow, Johnny was already down the hill searching the ditch, flinging cart parts onto the road. "Look at this junk."

Our beautiful cart was spread all over the place. Some pieces just disappeared. One of the wheels must have flown into the woods because we never found it. The cockpit was busted in two, and there wasn't a thing left that even remotely resembled our engineering masterpiece.

Larry said, "Look at your arm. Man, what a crash."

The doll pillow, taped to my left arm, was gone, and there was gravel sticking to shreds of friction tape hanging from my elbow. Three of the five layers were scraped away, loose ends heavy with sand and small rocks.

"What the heck happened?"

"I dunno. All of a sudden, the rope broke. Man, I thought I had it made. We shoulda' used stronger rope. Did you see how fast I was goin? I'll bet I set a speed record. Where's the wheels? If we had bigger wheels, I bet I could'a made it."

Johnny rejoined us, and we spent considerable time debating what went wrong. Everybody checked me for broken bones; Ronnie's mother was a nurse, so he asked the most questions. His nose bubble had receded, once again, to a glob.

It wasn't long before we moseyed off in the direction of the dump, intent on finding bigger wheels for a new cart.

CHAPTER 13

Autumn on the Island

As autumn settled in, the leaves and swamp grasses began to lose their luster. Twilight, stretching far into the night during earlier weeks, now seemed eager to turn to darkness, and the crisp mornings forced us to wear our tennis shoes when we went outside.

While the evenings remained warm, there was a change in their makeup; chilly dampness that had been missing for the past several months required us to wear light jackets while playing after dark. The neighbors began to stay inside during the evening, and daytime would find the parks nearly vacant. Dawn often lay under a dense fog, not disbursed by the sun until mid-morning, and there was a frantic nature exhibited by all the critters.

Squirrels raced around tree trunks, one chasing another, and they could be seen scampering here and there with acorns filling their mouths. Fall was the time of year when they fortified their nests with fresh, green branches gnawed from the main tree.

With the shortened days, our games of statue-maker and kick-the-can followed suit, and our late night games of flashlight tag and capture-the-flag were stopped altogether.

But…there was the occasional warm evening, and we found a new way to fill our time.

Growing in the low area at the bottom of the hill in front of our house was a nearly impenetrable vine network of wild cucumbers. While they were different sizes, most were two or three inches long and about an inch in diameter. They looked like they would hurt, with spines covering the outside, but they were soft with a spongy body and light enough to prevent serious injury. When picked at the perfect time, they were filled with moisture, and we could throw them with accuracy.

We started by forming teams; the one I preferred was when Larry, Dickey, and I went against Johnny, Ronnie, and however many of Larry's sisters wanted to play. It was long-range warfare, pelting cucumbers across the road with the intent of hitting someone on the other side. When lucky enough to connect, they would split and deliver a wet blow.

Pitching cucumbers across the road, we had to stop every time a car came along. Hmmm. The mind began to turn.

I think it was Dickey who took the initiative. Everyone held their fire as a car drove between us billowing dust from the loose gravel and sand on the road. Splat! I saw it hit on the edge of the rear bumper, as the car continued without pause.

"Nice throw!" Larry was concealed somewhere between Dickey and me. "Did you see that sucker splatter?"

An immediate timeout was declared while we discussed the potential of this new sport. Gathering on the roadside, it was soon apparent that with in-depth discussion came unwanted criticism and warnings from the girls. Not wanting to appear timid, each of the boys declared our bravery and pledged to splat every car that passed. Ronnie made the pledge, but realized his mother expected him home at any minute—would we please excuse him.

That was when the girls left.

That was when we should have left with them.

We took our positions. Larry and I were on one side of the road while Dickey and Johnny hid on the other.

"Here comes one!" I could hear the excitement in Dickey's voice.

The car was coming down the hill in front of my house and was going at a pretty good clip. Anticipation ruled as I hunkered inside the vine patch.

The car drew closer. My heart beat faster. Stay down, stay down, not yet, hold it—the car was now within 20 yards. Stay down, wait, wait, wait.

As it drew even with us, Larry and I popped up and threw with all our might. Splat, splat. We were on the passenger side of the car and below road level, making it impossible for the driver to see us, not so with the two on the other side of the road.

As the car moved beyond us, I saw Johnny poised to throw, apparently waiting a little too long to make his move. Behind him, Dickey was making a hasty retreat to the woods that bordered the rear of the swampy area. There was a cloud of dust, and gravel flew as the driver hit the brakes.

Johnny, looking confused, completed his throwing motion, unable to stop and not knowing for sure whether he dared finish the job. That's the last I saw before dropping into the center of the vine patch.

I heard shouts as the driver jumped out of his car and charged toward where Johnny had been when he threw the cucumber. From the bordering wood line, I heard Dickey. "Run, Johnny, run."

I can only imagine the scene: the driver charging into the swamp, Johnny running as fast as he could to reach the woods and Dickey's voice.

"Get back here, you little rat! When I get my hands on you, you'll wish you never threw that thing. You little punk." I could hear his voice moving in the direction from which Johnny had thrown. I heard nothing from Johnny, but I could see him in my mind's eye, running as though his life depended on it, which of course, it did.

"You little..."

I heard a muffled exhale, and the crashing of underbrush and swamp grass being crushed as he took a tangled header.

"You little—! You rotten little—!" I heard him climbing back unto the road and heading to his car. "If I ever catch you, you'll wish you were never born."

I heard him walk around the car, gravel crunching beneath his shoes. Then he stopped, and muttered something about "more of em," and I could only assume he saw the splats delivered by Larry and I. The gravel crunched as he walked directly toward where I was hiding.

Whoa, this could be a problem.

I heard him enter the grass, only feet from where I lay. I imagined him looking in every direction, trying to find a clue, wanting to pound bumps on someone for having the audacity to throw stuff at his beautiful car. Eventually, he turned, left the swamp, and crossed the road toward his idling vehicle. The door closed, followed with a slight grinding as he put it in gear, and the wheels slowly turned on the gravel. He gradually picked up speed until I heard the squeaking of brakes when he approached the stop sign at Swenson's corner.

I met Larry in the middle of the road, where we celebrated our success with a victory dance and giggles, not noticing the car now approaching from the corner—until he hit the gas and gravel flew.

Larry screamed, "He's coming back!"

That was enough for me. I took off like a rocket for the little hill that bordered the small swamp. Darkness was beginning to settle in, and I didn't spend a single moment wondering where my friends were. My concentration was focused on getting to the screen porch, quickly, safely, and without a stranger bursting in on my heels.

It was like the devil was chasing me as I raced up the front steps, grabbed the screen door, and yanked it open. I flew through the opening and was in the middle of the living room before the door slapped shut behind me.

I stood there, body heaving, gasping for air.

"Dale, what in the world?" Mom was seated on the couch, mending dad's socks.

"I just ran from Bursch's to see how fast I could go." No mention of our encounter with the man in the car.

"You shouldn't get so out of breath; it's not good for you."

"I know, Ma. I just wanted to see how fast I could get home."

"Look at your shirt! Where in the world have you been? The whole back is ripped. What have you kids been doing now?"

I peeled the shirt over my head and held it in front of me. Sure enough, there was a sizable three-corner tear in the back. The front was dirty from playing and had multiple dried splat marks where I had gotten nailed with well-aimed cucumbers. I had no idea how the tear occurred.

"Just playin by Bursch's." Safely at home, I now needed to avoid more questions from an inquisitive mother. I turned and headed for the back bedroom, where I could change into my pajamas.

"You wash up first; you're not going to bed dirty."

I went to the bathroom and washed the ground-in dirt from my elbows. I left, safe from the dangers presented by the darkness outside, and headed for the back bedroom, tossing my torn shirt down the basement stairs as I passed. My dirty clothes, from days past, littered the floor at the bottom of the steps, awaiting mom's washday. I grabbed my pajamas from the top drawer, slipped them on, and headed for my bed on the front porch. Mom, as usual, came to tuck in the loose edges.

It was almost possible to gauge the time of year by the quantity and makeup of the blankets. The September blanket arrangement usually included a couple of extra wool covers, and by mid-October, I had at least four inches of thickness covering me; the heaviness of their combined weight felt wonderful and guaranteed I would remain warm until morning.

With that thought, I drifted off to sleep.

It was quite a while before we worked up enough courage to splat cars again, but as with all things, time seemed to heal, and a scar had developed, which made the fear I felt as I ran home fade from my mind. In its place, I was once again, filled with the daring of innocence and a complete belief in immortality. I would continue to press the limits of good taste with my friends, and we would find new ways to enjoy our childhood.

Tomorrow would be a beautiful new day.

CHAPTER 14

Thanksgiving

My direct family was small. My dad's only brother had died at twenty-seven, leaving two little girls and a third born nine days after he died. They moved to Rapid City a short time later.

My mother had a sister who stayed in the area. That was it. I had two boy cousins while growing up, and every summer, my Rapid City girl cousins would come to our house, which was always memorable and greatly anticipated because they drew boys like flies to honey.

But, the most special times in my childhood involved my Auntie Lailah, Uncle Bud, and my two cousins Terry and Brooks.

My aunt was beautiful, inside and out. She brought a bubbly and iridescent presence that would light up any room. She was my favorite person.

Uncle Bud never worked for anyone else after his father died. For a time, he owned and ran, Hilltop House in Glenwood, primarily a bar that served food. He later bought a small café in Eden Valley: Coe Café was where we, most times, went to celebrate Thanksgiving.

About 65 miles from our home in Island Park, we made the trek each year. I loved it. At the café, which they closed to the public on

Thanksgiving Day, we had access to the special freezer. It sat on the floor behind the counter and had two pairs of lids, hinged in the middle, allowing access to the left or right. Inside were round cardboard cylinders filled with the smoothest ice cream in the world. One had vanilla, another chocolate, and yet others with every kind of goodness and color known to man. We were allowed one scoop of our choice.

* * *

"Auntie Lailah, auntie Lailah can we have an ice cream cone?"

"Of course you can."

A mad race to the freezer with my mother's voice trailing, "You know the rule, Dale. One scoop" This was the only place we were allowed to scoop our own, and I always considered the choice with great care. "Brooks, what's this, what's this, what's this," pointing from one cylinder to the next as I worked my way through the choices. Most times, I settled on chocolate-chip.

The scoop itself was an engineering marvel, a round metal cup with a straight handle, perfect for scooping. A thumb-operated lever connected to a thin piece of metal shaped to fit in the cup completed the magic. When the lever was depressed toward the handle, the metal strip followed the contour on the inside of the cup, and the ice cream plopped out of the scoop with a perfectly rounded bottom.

Tables were set up, buffet-style, in the open space between the counter and booths lining the opposite wall. There was Turkey with all the fixings, a massive bowl of thick, rich gravy, and a large platter of stuffing. I never understood the stuffing and didn't see much value in soggy chunks of bread, but the adults ate it like there was no tomorrow. There were cranberries, pickled herring, gobs of mashed potatoes, and sweet potatoes too. We had mince and pumpkin pies, apple pie, and one time we had a peach pie. That one didn't go over too well. I figured we had every kind of food known to man. Since Uncle Bud was a hunter and fisherman, there was always a goose and smoked fish to complete the offering.

Nut season started at Thanksgiving and ended after Christmas. Auntie Lailah had two wooden bowls filled with different kinds of nuts. Brazil nuts, which were the hardest to open, walnuts, pecans, and filberts. Each bowl had two nutcrackers and pointed probes to help pry the meat from the shell. When new, the metal nutcrackers worked like a charm, but after the small spring used to align the handles broke, they were another story.

While the men had access to and enjoyed uncle Bud's famous eggnog, we were always allowed to help ourselves to the non-alcoholic version placed alongside the high-test stuff.

It was always cold outside, and it seemed that Auntie Lailah had the heat cranked to about 95 degrees. No matter how nice I looked when I arrived, I always ended up in my T-shirt.

The café had a living space at the rear. Brooks slept in a bed placed in a narrow room separating the restaurant from the slightly larger room that served as an adult bedroom and living space. Brooks' bedroom doubled as storage for things used to run the café. Although small, it had plenty of nooks and crannies for us to play hide-n-seek.

With the announcement that dinner was ready, everyone ambled to the café seating area and taking a plate, walked the line filling them with our choice of offerings. Auntie Lailah was flitting about, refilling platters with more meat, potatoes, and that confounded stuffing. Mom came by and refilled my plate with more mashed potatoes and gravy, which I ate with gusto. Then it was pie time.

My favorite was apple. Auntie Lailah made the greatest pie. The apples were so ripe they almost turned into a sauce, and she sprinkled the crust with sugar, baked crisp and thin, just the way I liked it. It billowed over the filling like a sweet parachute, dimpled where the tiny slice expanded to allow the steam to escape during baking. Fabulous pie.

There is one year in particular that stands out in my mind about Thanksgiving at Coe Café in Eden Valley.

* * *

"Twenty-three, twenty-four, twenty-five. Here I come ready or not."

I climbed from the booth, knowing exactly where to look. Sneaking to the opening at the end of the counter, I carefully peered behind. Umm, no Brooks. Well, he finally smarted up. Check the bathrooms—still no Brooks. I knew there was no place for him to hide in the cooking area so I checked the rest of the places he could be, under the bed, behind the chair, under some blankets stuffed in a corner.

Wow, he found a good spot this time. Thinking I could sneak up on him, I quietly prowled the area. I even stood on Auntie Lailah's trunk to slide the curtains and look on the shelves in his bedroom, which he shared with food storage—still no Brooks.

"Dinner is served, come on boys it's time to eat."

I jumped off the trunk and raced to fill my plate. Of course, I was last in line, so I made the rounds, taking what looked good, and settled in a booth to begin my feast.

"Where's Brooks?"

"Umm, I dunno'."

"BROOKS. Come in here and eat." No reply.

"Dale, where's Brooks?" Mom sounded edgy.

"I dunno', Ma. Can I have more pie?"

"Dale, where is Brooks?" She now sounded angry. "Where did you leave him?" Yeah, definitely hostile.

"I dunno Ma, he's hidin' someplace."

"What do you mean, hidin' someplace?"

"We were playing hide-n-seek. He found a really good spot. I couldn't find him."

Things got real active then as the search for Brooks began in earnest. We checked every inch of that building, but no Brooks; that's when they turned on me.

Dad picked me up and plopped me on the trunk, where I sat, legs dangling over the edge, and the interrogation began.

"Where were you playing? Did he go outside?"

Auntie Lailah's face began to turn pale gray, and I could feel tears building as my breathing became ragged.

"Dale, this is serious. Where were you two playing? Stop kicking the trunk."

My aunt was racing around looking for a coat; my mother was already at the door.

"I'm not kickin' the trunk."

Dad's eyes blinked as he watched my feet dangling loosely. The kicking sound continued.

He snatched me from the trunk, undid the latch, and opened the top.

Up popped Brooks, sweat dripping from his chin, hair disheveled, madder than a hornet.

"Why'd ya leave me in there, ya stupid clod."

Auntie Lailah grabbed him by the arm, yanked him from his hiding spot, the best hiding spot ever, and smacked his butt. Dad grabbed me by the arm and smacked my butt. Brooks and I were both crying and left to think about it while the adults marched back to the feast.

I remember hearing a click when I got on the trunk, probably setting the latch. I don't remember much about the rest of the day, but I do remember the silent treatment. There was no more ice cream, no more pie, and no more anything.

I guess I should have found him before I ate.

* * *

Thanksgiving Day always featured a football game. After everyone had eaten their fill, the standard routine was for the men to retire to the living area where Uncle Bud and Auntie Lailah had the television set. The Detroit Lions seemed to be the team I remember as being featured while they played other teams in their conference. Often it seemed that the Dallas Cowboys was their competition.

Because of the distance from the TV signal source, reception of the game picture was subject to weather conditions and often drifted from clear, to a rolling picture, to a zigzag picture. I remember the men adjusting the antenna, placed on top of the set by twisting and turning and changing the angle until the image cleared.

For some reason, one visit, in addition to our hide-and-seek Thanksgiving, sticks in my mind.

Just east of the café was a bait store. The name of the place escapes me, but Brooks and I sometimes visited there. I remember the store as being equipped with the standard rows of fishing equipment; artificial lures, sinkers, rods, and reels. Like any good bait store, they also sold worms, grubs, and minnows of various sizes.

Included in this store were all sorts of ice fishing equipment. The owner also sold hand-made decoys used to attract larger fish, Northern Pike, Walleye, and those that could be taken with spears. This sport was strictly a winter affair. The spear-house was windowless and placed over a large rectangle cut from the ice. With a hole in the floor, usually 3x3 or 3x4, it provided a portal to the depths, one large enough to allow a person to sit in comfort, spear in hand, watching the action below. The hand-made lure was lowered into the water on a thin line. Attached to the decoy were metal strips to act as fins dictating the movement of the bait when raised and lowered in the water.

The thing I remember was watching the store's owner carving the decoy and attaching the metal fins. In particular, I remember him pouring molten lead into a carved hollow to weight the thing to drop as far as the line allowed. By occasionally raising and lowering the bait, the metal fins directed it in a circle.

* * *

All in all, Eden Valley holds many memories from my past. Not only was it our halfway stop when Dad took me hunting in the fall and on our returns from the weekend, but it also is the source of many Thanksgivings with my family.

CHAPTER 15

Old Man Winter

The four of us, Larry, Ronnie, Johnny, and I had been playing together most of the day. We were buddies, blood brothers in the real sense, sealed by ceremony using buckthorn to draw and share samples.

It was November, and in the midst of the warmest dose of Indian Summer those parts had seen in years. At 12:30, the mercury topped out at 77 degrees. Since then, it had dropped like a rock. Now at 1:45, it was riding 63 and dropping fast. One thing about fall in Minnesota, the weather could change on a dime, and it was doing just that as we drew even with Einer Swenson's house.

"Hey, let's see if we can pick a few wild grapes."

Einer Swenson had two things nobody else on the island had, at least as far as we knew. Einer Swenson had grapes, and Einer Swenson had pears.

He had an honest to goodness pear tree that drew kids like an ice cream truck; only this time of year the pears were long gone, victims of theft, and Amy Swenson's pantry. But, the grapes were still on the vines climbing the line of cedars behind Swenson's house.

The vines were so thick they caused the top ten feet of the trees to bend in a graceful arc. How could any red-blooded American boy resist climbing to the top?

Well, we figured there was no reason to resist, except good sense, and our parents were far enough away to make good sense a missing commodity.

Up we went.

It didn't take long for the novelty of just hanging thirty feet in the air to wear a little thin. "Come on, let's get 'em swayin'." Larry was to my right, while Johnny was at the top of the tree on my left. Ronnie, safely on the ground, had no shortage of advice and made sure he wasn't left out. In spite of his coaching, it was hopeless. We couldn't work together if our lives depended on it, and the result was a shaking of the trees in uncoordinated jolts.

"Hey, check this out. I'm Tarzan king of the jungle."

I looked to my right and was amazed to see Larry draped across a network of vines. He was a good two feet away from any stable branches, and he appeared to be floating in the air.

"Wow, neat." Johnny wasted no time in testing the vines that twisted among the branches on his tree. The problem was, Johnny was a little heavier than Larry, and the vines on his tree were just a little thinner.

"How 'bout this." He leaned out from the main trunk, his backside cradled in a network of vines. "I'm sittin' on the living room couch." He folded his arms across his chest and leaned back, the strong vines holding him within arms reach of substantial branches.

Without warning, the vine carrying most of his weight slipped.

"Eyee-yikes" His eyes bugged as he snapped his arms toward the now unreachable trunk, and I heard him mutter, "Holy Mary, Mother of God…"

The vines held, and Johnny stopped his prayer, and his fall, after only six inches. Gingerly he reached out, and closing fingers around the nearest branch began pulling his body toward safety. His legs were trembling.

"Ha, ha, Johnnie. Scared the crap out of ya, huh?" Ronnie, watching from outside the stand of cedars, made the most of it.

"Hey, I'll bet I can transfer to your tree." Jonny's reaction to near-death buoyed my confidence. Surely, I could make a better showing than he did. Larry scrambled to the safety of stable branches where he turned toward me.

"You crazy? That must be six feet. You'll never make it." Larry spoke with unveiled concern, which was a little surprising to everyone. Usually, Larry didn't give a rip about anybody.

Johnny, a little too eager to have someone join him in failure, said, "Aw shoot, that oughta be an easy jump."

I figured I could make it, no problem. As I sized up the distance and placed my feet on the thickest branch I could find, a small doubt began to trickle into my brain. Oh well, I gotta' do it now. "Here goes."

I could picture the leap, like a great African cat, unstoppable.

As I launched from the tree, I was about to learn a couple of universal truths. The first: the relationship between action and reaction. As I pushed off, the tree moved to the rear. Instead of a graceful leap, I felt myself for a short moment, hanging in space. That's when I learned the second universal truth: gravity.

I hit the ground with a resounding thump.

"You all right?"

"Huh?" My ears were ringing, and I had trouble focusing.

"Holy cow." I could hear Ronnie from the other side of the bushes. "You dropped like a bag of rocks. How the heck you didn't kill yourself is somethin. Man, are you lucky. I wish I had a movie of that one. Man, what a fall."

I sat there for a few minutes, waiting for everything to stop spinning and the ringing to end. After satisfying myself that I was in one piece, we crawled through the bushes to open ground on the edge of the tree line where Ronnie waited. Once there, we heard in great detail how fantastic my fall was, and how stupid I was, and what I should have done, and on, and on, and on. Ronnie's perpetual nose bubble was prominent.

Larry was the first to notice. "Dang…I should'a wore a long sleeve shirt. Ya think it's gettin' cold?"

"Yeah, it's raining, and it sure is gettin' colder.

We stepped outside the cedar overhang and held out our hands to test for raindrops, looking very official, our arms glistening and water dripping from our elbows.

"Yep, it's rainin' alright. Probably ought to head out." My official proclamation, based on research conducted on-site.

Ronnie bid farewell and struck out for his house.

Johnny's house was on the way, and Larry and I left him with a wave and a promise to come calling when it stopped. Larry's house was next. I left him there, and as I walked up the hill toward home, I could feel the chill and begin to see clouds of exhaled breath.

Within an hour, the first snow of the season began to fall, small flakes, drifting with the wind currents, too light to accumulate, melting on contact. In another hour, the flakes turned to globs large enough to remain visible for a time after landing. It started to collect on the oak leaves, creating small platters of white snow ringed with jagged crimson lanyards from the leaf beneath.

Another hour passed, and the front yard had a thin white cover.

By the time we ate dinner, the wind had come up, making the gently falling flakes whip into a frenzy of horizontally driven pellets that peppered the windows and slammed into the screens of the front porch. Mom had moved me into the back bedroom, just off the kitchen, and by the time I went to bed, flakes were blowing in whirlpools past the dining room window.

The island was in the grip of an early-season blizzard.

As we slept, the terrible wind screamed its fury, and by midnight, there were six inches on the ground. When dawn broke, Einer Swenson's homemade snow gauge was buried beneath a six-foot deep snowdrift extending the length of his house.

I awoke and lay there for a while, letting the fog of sleep dissipate.

I wonder how much snow we had? Yesterday was Sunday. That means today's a school day. Wow, maybe school's canceled.

I jumped out of bed and raced into the kitchen, where Mom was making breakfast. WCCO was in the process of announcing school closings, and I listened with great interest when they got to the M's.

Then I heard it, "Mound School District 85—closed.'" My heart soared, and my mind raced. This was great. Not just delayed for two hours, but closed—for the entire day. I couldn't wait to get outside and survey the damage.

I looked out the front window and saw only a hump where Dad's car was parked. It was impossible to see where the yard ended, and the road began. The distance between our house and Dickeys was as flat as a tabletop, with no hint of where the road lay under the white blanket, no dip at his front yard, no trace of driveway or stairs. Flat. White.

"Wow, I gotta go out."

Mom was way ahead of me. She dug out my winter coat and over-shoes, the ones with the tops of the toes worn thin as Kleenex from dragging during last year's sledding. Wool snow pants, a little tighter than last year, three wool shirts, a couple of pairs of wool socks over my high-top tennis shoes, the combination stuffed into 5-buckle overshoes, my wool cap, the one with a brim and earflaps that tied under my chin, and I was almost ready. The last was wool gloves covered by black and white striped wool mittens; themselves tucked into leather bags with thumbs. We knew these as chopper mitts.

Finally, a good 15-minutes later, Mom topped it off with a scarf around my neck, and I was ready. It's amazing that I could move, trussed up as I was.

The direction of the wind the night before kept the snow from drifting in front of the screen door on the front porch, and I had little trouble forcing it open enough to squeeze through.

Once outside, things changed drastically. I knew there were steps from the door to the yard, but they'd disappeared. I shuffled forward until I found the edge of the top step and worked my way to the bottom. The snow was up to my waist, and with every step I took, it got deeper, forcing me to kick with my feet and scoop with my hands.

Geez, it was gettin' a little warm.

I worked at it for about 20 minutes, finally retracing my steps back to the screen door to get a full view of my progress.

Darn, all that work, and I was only about halfway to the road.

Sweat was burning my eyes, and balls of snow were dangling on the ends of my scarf. Someplace out there were my chopper mitts, earlier discarded because my hands were sweating. The red color of my wool gloves was barely visible under tiny balls of snow.

Maybe I should rest awhile—gettin' a little thirsty...man, am I hot.

I squeezed back through the screen door and let myself in the house. Mom, eyes rolling towards the ceiling, met me at the front door.

"Where are your mittens"?

"Umm... outside someplace.'"

Again, eyes rolled upward.

Undressing took roughly half as long as putting the stuff on. Now it was off to the bath. Imagine 9:30 in the morning, and I'm sitting in the tub. The reason was: "so you don't get chilled from all that sweating and such." I could never figure out how much sweat was required to warrant a bath, but I had to admit it felt pretty good.

* * *

I watched from the window as Dad shoveled a path from the front steps to the corner of the driveway, then working his way around the car and toward the basement door. It was a good hour before he came back into the house for coffee and toast that Mom had ready. About 30 minutes to regroup, and he was out the door again.

He had just walked to the back of the car when I heard the snowplow. Al Boll, the man at the wheel, the Iceman in the summer and plow master in the winter, was also the year around fire chief for the island volunteers. Aaah, the volunteers. These guys took pride in what they did, and they took it very, very seriously. My Dad and Mr. Boll were good friends, but it seemed that once in the dump truck with the snowplow attached, Al Boll turned maniac.

I saw him as he made the crest of the hill, heading toward the driveway. I could almost hear a gleeful chuckle as Boll gripped the steering wheel a little tighter, scrunching his shoulders forward in anticipation of the next few seconds.

Dad's mouth dropped open, and Boll's jaw took on a resolute jut.

When he got to within fifteen feet of the driveway, you could hear the engine rev as Boll shifted gears. When he drew even with the driveway, snow was flying from the plow blade, a good ten feet off both sides.

Dad jumped behind the car in time to miss being caught in the avalanche of plowed snow, but Boll had done his damage. There was now a five-foot ridgeline across the front of the entire driveway, and it took another 45-minutes to clear it away.

After Boll's pass, possibilities for sled runs opened up, and I couldn't wait to go outside again.

"Ma…can you help me find my sled?" Last year, Santa had given me a beauty.

She had an armful of laundry. "Dad always puts the winter stuff in the furnace room. Look there. I've got clothes to wash."

Sure enough, Dad had stored the sled behind the furnace. I pulled it out, wiped it down, removing seven month's worth of dust, and put it outside the basement door.

Mom was busy washing clothes, so I got myself ready, neglecting half the items worn earlier. I left through the front door, out the screen porch, and down the front steps, following the path Dad cleared to the driveway. He had gone to work, leaving a snowless rectangle in the driveway where the car was parked. Following the path he shoveled to the basement door, I retrieved my sled and trudged out the driveway to the road, heading for my friends' homes.

First, I called for Larry, then Johnny. After picking up Ronnie, we headed back to my house. Pulling our sleds four abreast on the plowed road, we split to allow the occasional car to pass, noting with satisfaction the slipping and sliding that took place as they climbed the hill in front of us. Heck, some of them even had to get a second run to make it.

The whole gang knew this only packed the snow, and made for a faster ride.

This was going to be a great winter.

* * *

There were a couple of things that everybody knew growing up in Minnesota. You don't touch any metal with anything wet, like your tongue, and you have to watch for bare spots in the road. This was Ronnie's first winter on the island. We figured it must not have gotten below freezing in Cleveland, because Ronnie didn't seem to know the rules. To top it off, with his perpetual snotty nose, he had developed the habit of wiping it on anything he saw available, usually his sleeve. Rocketing down the hill required both hands on the steering bar, so his tongue was working overtime to clean the upper lip. He was doing about 80 when he hit it.

Johnny was standing right there and described the scene for us with Broadcast Host clarity.

"He was flyin' by, tongue working his upper lip. It made contact with his sled metal about the time he hit the gravel. Don't know why it didn't get ripped off, cause it looked like it was stuck tight when the sled stopped. He just kinda slid right off the front."

It turns out, it was Ronnie's lucky day because his tongue didn't have time to freeze solidly, just enough to hurt a little. Ronnie learned a pretty good lesson.

* * *

We started from the front yard, sled at the ready, and sprinted forward, flopping on our bellies and racing onto the road, cutting sharply through the opening in the ridge and flying down the hill into the hollow. Sometimes we could get up enough speed to coast far into the swamp.

At least that's what we remembered from last year.

The problem was, just after leaving the road and jetting down the first few feet of the steep hill, the snow got a little deeper. After a couple of face-first slides and packing snow into loose sleeves and jacket necks that weren't zipped tightly, somebody had a 'duh' moment. Go down the hill sitting up, our feet on the steering bar would keep us from sliding off the front. Sitting up turned out to be the perfect answer to the deep drifts scattered on the hill. When one of us launched from the top, we reached warp speed in nothing flat. When we got to the inevitable drift, snow flew, and we cleared another few feet.

A couple of hours later, we had the run cleared, and other kids started showing up. Soon the snow was trampled, and we could go almost anyplace on the hill.

One of those that joined us was Billy McGinn. Billy lived closer to Avalon and was younger than we were, but a real daredevil, a trait that sometimes landed him in hot water. There was one slope in the hollow that was a little steeper than the regular sled runs, and Billy, sitting up on his sled, was poised at the top.

"Billy! Don't go down that side. You'll kill yourself!"

Either he didn't hear me, or...he figured he could handle it, either way, he was moving and headed for the ash tree about halfway down.

It was like a slow-motion car crash. When the sled made contact, he kept going, slamming into the tree at about thirty miles an hour. He was in the middle of a yell when his face met the bark, and his arms and legs whipped around the trunk.

We raced to the scene where he lay on his side with moans and unfocused eyes.

"Wow...Billy, you okay?"

"Ohhh."

We figured we better get him home, so we laid him on a sled and pulled him the three or four blocks to his house where we handed him over to his Mom with a succinct description, replete with details from the launch till near-fatal crash. Later examination of the scene showed the nick where the sled made contact. Above that, where his face met the bark, was a blot of frozen snot.

I guess he had a headache for a week or so, but he lived to slide another day.

CHAPTER 16

The Adams Boys

When I was nine or ten, I was the best snow cave builder on the face of the earth. Small and skinny, a huge advantage for that line of work, I could dig like nobody's business. Grab Dad's small coal shovel, and search out the perfect pile, usually at the corner of the driveway, and have at it. It never really registered that every cave I made could only accommodate one kid at a time, and it's not like they were lined up to crawl in and lie under a pile of cold snow, but occasionally a couple of brave souls would enter and lie there, nose to nose, and talk about how neat it was.

Sooner or later, someone would climb up the side and put their foot through the roof, leaving an unwanted chimney hole. With a little selective cutting and flinging of snow, we transformed the cave into a walled fort. Now there was something truly useful.

We fought epic battles in and around those forts, making legends and creating great welts on exposed cheeks. Our skirmishes were things of beauty. We established strict regulations: what constituted a killing shot, lob techniques, long-distance, and close-quarter fighting rules. Basically, everything necessary to conduct a proper war.

We lined the inner walls with cavities for storing our arsenal of ready snowballs, a bright idea that saved our bacon one particular Saturday afternoon.

* * *

FRONT: Dale Swanson, Susan Bursch, Darlene Bursch, Nancy Bursch
REAR: Betsy Bursch, unknown, Larry Bursch

We were prepped for battle, full coffers of ammo, and itching to get things rolling. The usual gang was there, this time joined by Dickey: Larry, Ronnie, Johnny, and Larry's sisters Darlene and Nancy. We had chosen sides for the battle about to unfold.

The sneak attack took us by surprise, sending our platoon into full retreat. Led by Gerald, the oldest Adams brother, the Adams gang charged into our midst flinging hard-packed snowballs at anything that moved. There were only four of them, but Gerald was older than we were and as merciless as a Hun.

We tried to fight but were no match for the well-organized Adams boys from over the hill. During the battle, Ronnie must have gotten a little confused and ran for home. Separated from the herd, he was captured, and the Adams boys retreated to the other side of the road to discuss their options and set the price for their hostage.

We regrouped around the fort at the corner of our driveway. The opposition hunkered down along the retaining wall by Dickey's house, tossing the occasional ice chunk into our group. We had to formulate a plan for beating them into submission and recapturing the hostage. It took us a while, but someone remembered our stash of fresh snowballs intact within the walls of the fort. We figured all we had to do was fill up with ammo, swing around behind the Adams boys, and pummel them from the hill behind their position.

The only glitch in the plan was figuring a way to carry enough ammo to the hill for a sustained attack. That was solved when I went into the basement and returned with the canvas Star Tribune bag that Dad carried papers in when he was a kid. The thing was perfect. It had a huge opening and was large enough to hold dozens of snowballs.

Dickey and I were to make a wide circle, come up behind the enemy, and beat them into submission, leaving Larry, Johnny, and Larry's sisters to keep the Adams boys busy while we made our approach.

Well, it worked like a charm. The gang lobbed snowballs into the Adams' camp, holding their attention, while Dickey and I circled, crawling the last few yards until we were within 20 feet from where Ronnie was being held. We peeked our heads out of the snow, timed our shots, and let fly.

Dickey's aim was perfect, smacking Gerald on the back of the head, nearly knocking his stocking cap off. My shot sailed between two of them. Then the yelling started as we charged to within 10 feet, throwing snowballs and screaming at the top of our lungs. Darlene, Nancy, Larry, and Johnny were adding to the confusion, yelling, and lobbing snowballs. The Adams boys didn't have a chance. Taken entirely by surprise, they likely thought there was a whole army attacking.

Dickey and I pumped snowball after snowball at Ronnie's captors, keeping them too busy dodging missiles to retaliate. They took off down the road, snowballs exploding on the surface around them as the whole gang joined in the rout; a very satisfying result and one relived for the next couple of hours.

The Adams boys never came to that neighborhood for the rest of the winter. They probably figured it wasn't worth the risk.

CHAPTER 17

Christmas

A kid just knows when it's going to be a good Christmas, and a good Christmas is what every kid on the planet wants. This year, I set my sights on a Western Ranch Set. This extravagant expectation was set in motion a year earlier when my Aunt Margaret from Rapid City sent me the 'Boys Fun Book.' Toward the end of the book was the most magnificent set of ranch buildings, and horses and cowboys I'd ever seen. It showed a kid in pajamas, obviously Christmas morning, setting pieces in their appropriate places. It was branding time in the old corral.

The moment this year's package from her arrived, I knew what I had. A little shaking, tipping, and rattling revealed what lay inside the exquisitely wrapped box. The western ranch set was mine.

My Saturday mornings were total immersion in television and the B-westerns the box offered. If only I'd have put my mind to schoolwork as I did on those westerns, I would now be a Nobel Laureate—at least.

I knew every cowboy, most of their horses by name, and the thing that made them unique. Nowadays, that would be called the "hook." Tom Mix and Tony, the Cisco Kid, and Diablo. Lash Larue was handy with the whip, Tim Holt, the white ten-gallon hat and extraordinary peripheral vision, Buck Jones, Johnny Mack Brown, Hopalong Cassidy, and his horse Topper. Of course, the Lone Ranger and Tonto; Ken Maynard, Gene Autry, and my all-time favorite, who I love to this day, Roy Rogers and Trigger. With that kind of background, it's easy to see why I was excited about the ranch set.

My sister, Jill, had a talent that came into play every time there were presents in the house. She had the uncanny ability to unwrap a gift and rewrap with the same paper. When finished, the ribbon was in place, and nobody was the wiser. She was smart enough to select a single present, examine the contents, and replace it under the tree in the exact position as before the larcenous event took place.

This Christmas, I couldn't wait to get a glimpse of my brand new ranch set. After a few days of shaking and rattling, Jill informed me it was time to pick a gift to peek at before Christmas morning. We had become expert at feigning surprise on Christmas morning.

* * *

We retreated to the bathroom, locked the door, and began the task.

"C'mon, open mine first."

"Sorry...I've already got mine started."

I knew that was a lot of baloney because we just got there, but I sat patiently as she carefully removed the bow and undid the tape on her package. I was in awe of her abilities. She carefully removed the wrapping paper, being sure to note the corner folds to be duplicated during the rewrap. After at least a hundred and fifty hours of intense concentration, she removed the cover on the box inside.

"I knew it. I just knew it. It's the doll I wanted." I looked in the box to see a beautiful, blond-haired, blue-eyed baby, complete with a bonnet and ribbon tied under her perfectly shaped chin. She wore some kind of billowy gown with beautiful patent leather shoes. Jill never took the presents out of the box, just looked, and rewrapped, leaving some genuine surprise and joy for Christmas morning. She replaced the cover and the paper, slid the bow in place, and carefully put it aside.

My turn.

The excitement was so powerful I could hardly contain it.

It seemed like another hundred hours went by before she laid the paper aside.

"Go ahead; take off the cover."

"Man-o-man, wait till you see this, Jill. It's got a ranch house, corral, horses, cowboys, and all kinds of stuff." I gave it another shake just to figure it out before popping the lid.

Anticipation. I figured I'd at least examine the ranch house before we rewrapped it. My breath caught in my throat as I slowly lifted the lid.

It didn't register…no ranch house, no cowboys.

Inside the box that I held sacred, was my Rapid City gift.

Cookies.

Smashed and obliterated from all the shaking, now nothing but crumbs and a few remaining pieces large enough to rattle when I shook the box.

I sat there, staring into the crumb pile. Not a word. Total silence. I just stared into my box of crumbs.

I could hear something coming from Jill. A giggle? My eyes slowly left the precious container that moments earlier contained my fantastic ranch set, and found their way to my sister's face. Try as she may, she couldn't contain herself, covering her mouth with both hands trying to hold back the laughter bubbling up inside. We sat there for a while, gesturing, grinning at each other, stifled laughter fighting to come out.

And we ate cookie crumbs.

She took less care during the rewrap process, and I don't remember unwrapping the thing on Christmas morning, but a lesson had been learned.

Never associate a gift with one received a year earlier. It can be deadly.

CHAPTER 18

Snowballs and Boy Scouts

In the winter of 1952-53, my dad started Boy Scout Troop 201.

Winters were nearly as fun as summers. In place of pelting cars with wild cucumbers, it offered the opportunity to pelt cars with snowballs. The naked dirt cliff on the south side of the road from our house made a perfect ambush point. At least that's what we thought. We figured it would be impossible for anyone to catch us before we reached the safety of the woods, especially if we did the deed in the dark.

Well—we figured wrong.

* * *

Dickey and I crouched at the top of the hill, waiting for the car to reach the crest where it would be directly under the streetlight. We let fly, and both connected. The car slammed on the brakes, the door flew open, and the chase was on.

It took us a while to realize the guy was serious about catching us, so we were more than a little tardy in starting our mad dash for the woods. By the time we reached the first trees, he was at the ambush point, and a quick glance told me he intended to cause serious injury if he caught us. We were pretty small, and the deep snow bothered us a lot more than it did him, so he closed the gap…fast.

I darted left and right, from tree to tree, doing my best to keep them between us, while Dickey was doing the same, somewhere to my left. The guy must have been confused by all the tracks and paths made during earlier play because he stopped to get his bearings. I stood, immobile, behind the tree, hoping he would give up. Now well into the woods and out of reach of the streetlight, the darkness served as an ally. He never advanced further than where he stopped, but it seemed like an hour before he turned and walked to his idling car, put it in gear, and drove away.

That was it for the day. Dickey had disappeared, and I went home, already thinking about tomorrow and possibilities for the new day.

* * *

It was at this point in my life that my father started Troop 201. In retrospect, it was providential that dad would take that path. It suited him and permitted his influence to affect many boys from Island Park. Jim Wendt, a neighbor, younger than dad, enthusiastic, and with the ability to inspire in a more physical manner, joined him in the formation of Dad's troop.

As literature from the Boy Scout Viking Council periodically arrived in the mail, Dad left it in conspicuous spots where he figured I would see it. I took an interest and studied the books with a curiosity that soon turned to passion. Before long, he subscribed to Boy's Life, a scouting magazine aimed at scouting age kids. I was hooked. He began to allow me to go with him to the Tuesday night meetings, although not yet twelve, and too young to become a full-blown scout.

The original troop was formed with only six or seven kids who met periodically at the island's Village Hall. They were a pretty sedate bunch, good students intent on learning all they could about scouting, each striving for the next higher rank. One particular winter evening, something happened that changed the structure of the troop, and the group dynamics took on a new character.

The meeting had been dismissed, and my dad and Jim were tidying up when the door burst open, and the scouts flooded in. It turned out they were victims of an ambush by some big kids who peppered them with snowballs when they left the building. Jim went out to call off the volley but was driven back by a fusillade of well-packed snow. Jim called a quick meeting and sold the guys on a strategy to take the fight to the interlopers. He reasoned that an organized group could demoralize and defeat the gang outside.

One poor soul was delegated to be the decoy, and a briefing commenced. With a plan in place, he turned the lights off, and the troop gathered at the side door. I don't remember who drew the short straw, but his job was to go out the front door where the enemy waited—to draw their attention.

The decoy made his move. Sure enough, he was peppered with snowballs, and his screams to stop drew the attention of the remaining antagonists, who, sensing easy pickings, joined in the fun. The resulting preoccupation allowed the troop to charge out the side door uncontested. The action proved highly successful, and after a short battle, the enemy called for a truce.

Dad and Jim invited the attackers to the next meeting, and the troop's new identity began to emerge. No longer just intellectually strong, the new members brought athleticism to the group, and camaraderie of spirit.

Sometime during the winter of my tenth year, dad and Jim approached the troop with a proposition. They could work toward advancement, and if everyone progressed, there was a possibility of going for a week's trip to a scout camp in northern Minnesota.

The kids responded by working hard, and parents were contacted for their permission and monetary commitment.

Reservations for the troop to attend Many Point Scout Camp were made, and my summers for the next several years were cast.

My first year at Many Point was an introduction to the spectacular! Underage, I spent the week with my mom and little sister, Linda, at the family camp on the opposite side of Many Point Lake. It was there where I gained the knowledge attached to lake bathing, poison ivy, outdoor toilets, kerosene lanterns, and the brotherhood of mosquito slappers; all in all, a perfect introduction to wilderness living.

Paper drives, car washes, and area cleanup campaigns, were some of the ways the troop raised money for the following year at Many Point. There was also a change in leadership. Jim Wendt moved from the area, and Orville Neal took the job of assistant scoutmaster. Experience from the first trip provided insight into programs, requirements, and expectations at the camp. In my second year, Dad opted for the two-week adventure. The extended time meant the troop would participate in the camp-wide competitions held for the two-week campers.

Incessant begging by me (still underage for becoming a scout) resulted in my dad allowing me to join the troop for the second week. At last! I was free of the little kids on the family side of the lake and permitted to join the big boys.

They camped at the Sequoia campsite, the furthermost site from the administration center. Our drinking water was delivered every few days in 25-gallon, steel milk containers. The troop was assigned the job of building a platform to hold the containers when they were delivered, and they made a beauty.

I shared a tent with Dickey Swenson, the official bugler for the troop. Swenson was a stocky kid, and he took the responsibility seriously, performing "taps" to end the day, and reveille at first light. We slept in camp issued wall tents on cots, also supplied by the camp. Our gear: clothing, boots, and all personal items, was stored under our cots on logs arranged to keep them off the ground. The latrine was situated away from camp and required a short walk.

When I arrived at the campsite, everyone was excited about the upcoming events. There were two all-day competitions designed to test individual abilities and troop knowledge in various disciplines.

Adventure Trails, the first, was to test the troop on wilderness survival and practical skills: building a shelter, fire starting, using natural elements to create a sundial, plant and tree identification, first aid, etc. Individual scouts were organized into teams by the scoutmaster; each team, then chosen randomly by a counselor to participate in whatever task was to be accomplished, and the groups were sent off on the trail designed to test a particular skill. Leaders were kept back while their troop walked the path, accompanied by a camp counselor to score the team's expertise in solving their problem. The scores from each group were totaled and the troop with the top overall score was the winner of the competition.

Our troop was well tutored because Dad had organized every weekly boy-scout meeting with an emphasis on solving problems, in many cases, identical to the ones being tested on Adventure Trails.

The night before the competition, Dad and Jim had chosen the group teams and identified a leader for each group. I remember being allowed to go with about five scouts from our troop, strictly as an observer. The trail we were on lead us to a person on the ground with a wire lying across his body. The counselor informed us that the wire was a result of a storm that had just passed, and the victim was unconscious. What should we do?

Assume the wire is live, and remove it with a dry branch—one is provided since the storm blew down live branches as well as one obviously dead and very dry branch. Next, verify that the victim is alive, send a person for help, determine the condition of the victim, and follow appropriate first aid steps.

At the end of the day, regardless of the problem encountered, every team was confident that they had made a strong showing.

The Lumberjack Rally was held on the second day and was the highlight of the summer. It was filled with athletic events associated with camp life. Every scout was required to participate in at least one event. Activities included rowing, canoeing, axemanship, tree climbing, archery, races, and many more tests of physical skills. Each contest was held in its own unique location, and the whole area was alive with boys as they rooted for their troop.

I was allowed to compete in the axemanship competition. The official placed a piece of string on a log, and we were expected to take a full swing, cutting the line as close to the middle as we could. The longer portion was discarded, and the process was repeated until the blow missed the remaining string. The scout that took the most whacks before missing was declared the winner. It was no surprise that I didn't come close to winning, but I did compete.

The other competitions were much more dependent on athleticism and things common to everyday life on Island Park. I don't think there was a single event that wasn't won by our troop. Tree climbing, no contest; relay racing through a wooded trail, no contest; rowing, no contest; canoeing, archery, swimming, it seemed we had at least one member of the troop that counted the event as his specialty.

The most spectator fun was with the canoe race. Again, members of our troop were raised on Island Park, a clear indication of familiarity with water sports. During this race, the director stood at the end of a dock, and participants stood with their canoes at the starting line. When the whistle sounded, each racer would push as far as they could, then mount the canoe and paddle to a buoy about fifty-yards out from shore. Upon reaching the buoy, they rounded it and paddled to the finish line at the dock.

There was a twist. Whenever the director blew the whistle, each contestant must vacate the canoe on one side, and climb back into the vessel on the other side to resume paddling. It was deafening when the shoreline erupted with boys cheering on their entry.

Island Park's Troop 201 finished before most others had reached the buoy. Many had capsized while others failed to reenter the craft.

To wrap up the camp experience a final campfire was attended by every troop participating in the two-day event. As each troop was announced, they marched to their preselected spot around the immense fire pit. Troop 201 marched into the campfire area to join troops from all over the country, with a cocky persona typical of a twelve-year-old fresh off a game-winning home run. It turned out we were worthy of that confidence. That was my first year when the troop won both events, and we were beside ourselves as my dad and Orville accepted the trophies.

Many Point Scout Camp loaded my brain with memories that I often revisit. Dickey Swenson, blowing reveille at dawn—in his underwear; gunwale pumping, P.I. baths with Fels Naptha soap, canoe trips to Ice

Cracking Lake and the Indian burial grounds, retrieved logging chains, Little Beaver Creek, and countless others.

One year we camped at Little Crow campsite, and Dick Bixley had an unknown critter visit his tent while we were out of the camp. No big deal, except it got into his stash of candy. After it happened a second time, he devised his plan. The solution was to borrow a live-trap from the conservation building. He figured he could trap the ground squirrel doing the dirty work and bring it far into the woods for release.

Well—He got the trap, and before we left for an organized activity scheduled for the entire morning, he loaded the trigger mechanism with candy and left, secure in the knowledge that the perpetrator would be captured and dealt with.

Upon our return, Bixley made a beeline for his tent. After opening the flap and a brief reconnaissance of the interior, he made a beeline away.

The word spread in an instant: BIXLEY HAD A SKUNK. A conference commenced, and the result was unanimous. It was Bixley's problem. Of course, there was no shortage of advice from the rest of us, and as I recall, poor Bixley, dressed like he was entering a hazmat environment, which he was, had not an inch of skin visible when he entered the tent. He exited, trap held at arm's length, and headed for the woods. Somehow, he avoided being sprayed and reentered the camp, victorious.

* * *

My final scouting experience was, again, shared with my dad. We went to the National Boy Scout Jamboree in Valley Forge, Pennsylvania, in 1958. During that trip, I got my first exposure to the East Coast, visiting New York City and Washington DC. Part of that trip included visiting Greenfield Village and the Henry Ford Museum in Dearborn, Michigan.

As with all my scouting experiences, the National Jamboree filled me with future memories, a scoundrel at the YMCA in New York City, tossing my shoes out the shower room window, forcing me to walk barefoot through Grand Central Station. Trading with a scout from Texas—a field mouse with self-applied charcoal stripes, passed off as a Minnesota gopher, for a Texas horned toad. I was awakened at midnight to answer citizenship questions while our train was crossing from Canada into New York State.

But, in addition to the meetings in the Island Park Village Hall and the National Jamboree, my scouting memories are of Many Point Scout Camp. Two weeks of many summers, which have turned into reruns, each viewing as enjoyable as the last.

Comment

There is one piece of my life that stands out in my memory as very special. Most of my childhood was woven around personal memories built from friendships with other people from my past. What follows are my recollections of special gifts given to me by my parents through their acceptance, involvement, and open approval of interaction with the wild critters living on the island. Their only stipulation was that I allowed them to come and go as each animal saw fit.

CHAPTER 19

Chips and Joe

L iving as we did, it was natural to encounter all kinds of wild animals. Roadkill was always exciting because it guaranteed a skin for my bedroom wall. Although my technique was a bit clumsy, using table salt to dry the skin, the resultant stiff pelt made a great wall hanging, and it didn't stink.

I don't know how my mother put up with my antics. She let me get away with things none of my friends' mothers would even consider. As a direct result of her tolerance, I attempted to rescue all kinds of wildlife or at least tried to rescue anything that still had breath. Birds could be a little tricky —more failures than successes—but there was the occasional healing. Every rabbit I brought home kicked the bucket. I was never able to nurse a rabbit back to health, partly because the only thing we could think to feed it was a clump of lettuce and a carrot. I never had one that even took a bite. Say goodnight, and the next morning it was stiff as a board.

The thing about running a MASH unit from our basement was the fact that once a commitment was made to try to save a life, that critter became exempt from ending up on the wall. I couldn't bring myself to slicing the skin off something that I once held while it was alive.

Me and Chips, The Gray Squirrel

For the life of me, I can't remember how we got Chips the Gray Squirrel. I remember having him while he was still red and hairless, and by using Mom's baby bottle technique and my sister Linda's doll bottle, we were able to get nourishment into his tiny body. As with the other baby animals I brought home, he grew at what seemed a frantic pace. It was as though overnight he grew into an adult.

Regardless of the wild thing, my mother was always adamant, give freedom, and let them decide to stick around. Pretty smart woman. It's similar to a puppy or a kitty cat. When they get hungry, they come to their master. The only difference is eons of domesticated conditioning.

I think that every animal has a consciousness that they rely upon for survival as well as an instinct for danger. Chips did a lot to lead me to this way of thinking. Every morning he would climb the screens and chatter until I let him in. He had the run of the house, going wherever he pleased.

He loved to climb on people, which is likely what made Mom fall in love with him. I saw him once sitting on her shoulder as she did her housework, altering his position to maintain balance when she bent to vacuum or stooped to dust the lower shelves.

Chips' time with us was cut short, not by death, but by another pet brought into the house, this one by my little sister, Linda. She brought home a kitten. A gift from a girlfriend, and a mortal enemy to the gray squirrel, it wasn't long before Chips no longer climbed the screens. However, the time that he was with us provided memories that pop to the surface from time to time.

* * *

My next pet stayed with us a little longer.

"Oh, Dale." My mother was obviously smitten by the tiny creature. "Where in the world did you find him?" She turned a suspicious eye. "You didn't rob him from his nest, did you?"

"No, Mom. Honest. I found him on the road. Ain't he neat?" I was lying through my teeth. I had indeed climbed to the very top of one of the tall pines that separated Turnquist's property from the road.

She held out her hands, and I transferred the small bird. With the movement, his enormous mouth snapped open as he tilted his head back.

"He seems to be hungry. Here, you hold him while I try to find the eyedropper." As I regained control of my treasure, I could feel his tiny feet pulsing in the palms of my hands as he continued to point his head upward, mouth wide open, entire body bobbing up and down.

A few minutes later, she returned with the eyedropper. "You hold him while I try to fix him something to eat."

I followed her to the kitchen, where she poured a little milk into a pan and placed it on the stove. "I think it should be warm before we give it to him." A short wait and multiple testing for proper temperature, and we were declared ready.

She loaded the eyedropper and drew it towards the baby in her left hand, moving the tip in front of his beak. Nothing. He sat, mouth closed. As though she had done it a million times, she tapped the edge of his closed beak, and it popped wide open. With great care, she poked the end of the eyedropper into his throat and squeezed the bulb—the tiny bird swallowed. I watched, fascinated, as she refilled the dropper and repeated the process. Before long, my mother had me feeding him.

"What's his name?"

"Gosh, I don't know. What kind of bird is it?"

"It's hard to say, but he looks like he is going to be pretty large when he grows up." She was examining him from head to toe. "Maybe we should wait with a name until we can see what he is."

That sounded good to me, so we decided to call him "Bird," at least for a while.

"When Dad gets home, maybe he can show you how to make a cage, so he has a place of his own. Meanwhile, I'll see what I can come up with for a nest."

She handed "Bird" to me and went to find something to put him in. As I sat at the kitchen table, the fact that I had stolen him from his nest was forgotten as I marveled at the tiny creature nestled in my cupped hands.

She returned with an old shoebox and one of my dad's wool socks, which she rolled and placed in the corner of the box to form a perfect nest. I carefully transferred him to his new home.

I was nearly beside myself, waiting for Dad to come home from work. Finally, he was there, and I showed him my treasure.

We set to work building a birdcage. We had no formal plans or drawings, but Dad was pretty good with his hands, and his imagination fueled our progress as it began to take shape. Together we built a masterpiece. A screened wonder, containing a swinging perch, a shelf for Bird to sit on, and enough room to stretch his wings as he grew.

We changed his diet to bread soaked in raw egg, which we initially poked into his throat with tweezers. He soon graduated to a small bowl with the mixture available for him to stab at whenever he wished. He was a voracious eater requiring food nearly every hour, and his jet-black feathers, which were becoming more apparent with each passing day, convinced us that he was a baby crow, very ugly but definitely a crow. That's when I decided his name would be Joe.

We placed Joe's cage on the desk in my bedroom with his shoebox on the shelf inside the cage. He loved it and in a few weeks, began to outgrow the shoebox. As he grew, his personality began to blossom. When we approached, he stood, mouth wide open, bobbing his head as though keeping time to a song.

Soon he began perching on the edge of his shoebox, flopping to the bottom of his cage when we approached. He loved it when I opened the door and put my hand in the opening. Hopping onto my outstretched fingers, he rode proudly as we paraded around the house. Before long, I learned I could leave the door to his cage open, and Joe remained inside until I approached.

I talked to him regularly when we were together, so he learned to recognize my voice. He was a quick study and soon recognized his name. A simple "Joe" caused him to hop out of his cage unto the desktop, flap his wings in a clumsy manner, and launch his round body unto the back of the desk chair. He was beginning to demand substantial food on a fairly consistent basis, so I was kept busy collecting small bugs for his meals.

One day Mom found a glob of "crow batter" running down the back of the chair and decided that Joe's days of sharing the back bedroom were over.

We moved the cage to the rear deck, placing it on a homemade stand designed to raise it to a convenient height—and he loved it. I left the cage door open during the day, and he hopped onto the edge of the stand, sitting for hours in the sunlight. At night, he retreated to his cage, and I shut the door, more to keep him safe from night critters than to confine him.

It was during this stage in Joe's life that he learned about blackbirds.

The morning sunlight streaming into the bedroom from the screened doorway shone and glittered off the small dust and pollen particles floating in the air. I heard the glorious pitch and trill of the Red-Winged Blackbirds as they screamed their joy for the new day. The gray squirrels were chattering while the smaller reds were bawling everyone out for daring to live in their space, which apparently, included the entire world. I stretched my arms, extending my legs and torso to stimulate every muscle while feeling the pleasant sensation of waking to the sweet sounds of summer and the incomparable smell that accompanied a summer dawn on the edge of the swamp behind the house.

As my body came to life, I hopped out of bed, exchanged my pajamas for swimming trunks, and stepped unto the deck.

"How ya doing, Joe? You ready to get out of there?"

Joe hopped to the closed door. I lifted the small hook and swung the cage door open, holding my hand as a perch, and Joe stepped onto my fingers. I raised him to my face, and, as he always did, he lightly rubbed his beak and forehead against my cheek. I stroked his head and placed him on the top of his cage. His head was now almost entirely black, with only a few of the fluffy, light-colored baby fuzz feathers that had so recently covered his entire body.

I heard my mother fixing breakfast in the kitchen.

With a final stroke, I said to him, "I'll be back as soon as I eat breakfast."

Joe stared unblinkingly. His eyes were as black as midnight as he cocked his head slightly to one side, while I retreated through the door.

Our proximity to the swamp, with all its pussy-willow bushes and bull-rushes, ensured a large population of Red-Winged Blackbirds. I loved their trill, and I loved their sheer numbers. I spent many hours flinging rocks in their direction, either by hand or with my slingshot, either method proving my accuracy to be far from brilliant. They appeared to recognize that danger was minimal. It was great sport; they seemed to enjoy swooping close and gliding to a nearby bush only to rocket skyward as a stone clattered in the nearby branches. However, they soon discovered the presence of our new houseguest, and life became a little more complicated for Joe The Crow.

"When do you think Joe will be able to fly?"

Mom, busy buttering my toast, "My guess is pretty soon. He's lost almost all his pin feathers; he's getting so handsome."

"How does he learn? Is it something that I can help teach him?" I was getting a little anxious to see Joe take to the air.

"Well, maybe you can coax him to flutter off the top of his cage. He'll eventually learn to go greater distances. I think he should try flying any day now." As she spoke, she turned from the sink where she was doing dishes.

"My, would you listen to those blackbirds. They must be madder than hops at something."

I stopped chewing, and I could hear the birds screaming their angry voices, a sound generally reserved for when one of the neighborhood dogs sniffed around the nesting bushes at the edge of the swamp. I got up and walked toward the deck. The closer I got, the louder the sound became until it sounded like hundreds of screaming birds. I approached the screen door, feeling my stomach tightening as I glimpsed shadows passing close. I timidly peeked at the rear deck.

No Joe! He was gone! In his place on top of the cage stood an arrogant, squawking blackbird, jumping left and right, mouth open, pointing his wicked head toward the base of the cage.

I felt fear and rage at the same time as I slammed the door against the outside wall and bolted through the opening. "Joe!" I screamed as I raced toward the cage, blackbirds scattering in all directions. "Joe! Here, boy." I waved my arms like a maniac dashing to the far side of the deck. The devil birds spread as they sought the safety of the nearby branches.

I turned, not knowing what I might see, afraid that Joe had been beaten to death by the marauders. There behind the stand, cowered Joe.

The black devils screamed their anger from the overhanging branches as I approached the frightened crow. I scooped him into my cupped hands. He was shaking as he prodded my palms with his feet and his tiny head with great big eyes tucked tightly against my body, as I carried him to the safety of my bedroom.

"Why did they do that?" Fear was beginning to overtake my anger. "What did he do to them?"

"That's the natural thing. Crows and blackbirds are enemies. They're just doing the natural thing." My mother had her arms around my shoulders as she spoke.

"How could they be so cruel?" I cried; my mind couldn't fathom what I had just witnessed.

"In nature, many things seem cruel to us, but it has been this way for thousands of years."

As I clung to the baby crow, my mother explained the natural conflict between the two families of birds. The blackbirds were protecting their territory from something they feared. She told me that crows would rob the nests when the babies were small, sometimes breaking the eggs and eating the babies before they hatched. They didn't do it to be mean. It was just what happens in nature.

"Well, they better not do that again."

My mother kissed my forehead and stepped toward the kitchen. "We'd better be more careful from now on; he's too little to protect himself."

I resolved to protect him from those nasty blackbirds for as long as necessary—or at least until he learned how to fly.

* * *

I worked with Joe every day, coaxing him to flutter from the top of his cage to the edge of the deck, and he began to get the idea. One day he maintained his flight long enough to overshoot the deck and flutter to the ground alongside the house. He was growing up.

There was another incident with the blackbirds, a result of Joe's new-found ability to stay aloft. He overshot the deck, but this time his flight path carried him on an angle, past the shed, and toward the swamp. The blackbirds swarmed as I raced to his rescue. I ran, half sliding down the steep hillside, as the blackbirds screamed and dove at the earthbound Joe. By the time I arrived, he had started to answer their agitated screeching with a mocking "Caw, Caw, Caw."

Soon Joe was flying from the top of his cage into the lower branches of the nearby trees. His initial flight almost ended in disaster when he carelessly banged into the trunk before settling on the extended branch. Within days, Joe was able to control his flight, and he began to extend his range. No matter where he flew or how long he was gone, I could step onto the back deck and loudly call his name. Joe would appear, gliding through the trees to land atop his cage. He considered the cage his home, and with the door now removed, he came and went as he pleased.

Then came the day I had been dreading. I awoke in the morning and went to greet the full-grown crow, which was our custom. The cage was empty. I called and called—no Joe. I called sporadically during the day but got no response.

Joe was gone. In his wake, he left me filled with memories. He provided hours upon hours of pure joy and learning. He exposed me to the laws of natural selection and survival of the fittest. He gave me pride and self-esteem that was priceless. The knowledge that I had raised the baby to an adult, and forged a bond with a wild bird, gives fulfillment that can't be equaled. Joe, my feathered friend, would always be with me. He remains as vivid in my memory as though our time together happened yesterday.

During the final days of my mother's life, we talked about our wild pets and the bonds that were formed during the time they elected to stay with us. The incredible depth of my mother's love astounds me to this day. Her patience and immense compassion revealed a deep-seated faith in God and the workings of the universe and taught me much about man's relationship to nature.

I am forever in her debt.

CHAPTER 20

The Last Wild Pet

Snoopy came to us on a Sunday afternoon, securely planted under the front seat of Bruce's car. Bruce was Jill's boyfriend, and earlier that day, he had gotten the baby raccoon from a farmer who found him while cutting trees.

About the size of a kitten, this little fur-ball had a tiny ringed tail and a mask over his eyes. His helplessness was apparent, and he looked frightened as Bruce carried him in cupped hands onto the porch.

"I'll bet he's hungry. What do coons eat?" I was firmly entrenched in the moment.

"Well, I'm not sure. Let's have a closer look at him." Mom picked up the baby in her right hand. "Why—look at this. This guy doesn't have any teeth yet.'" He squirmed and wriggled while she tipped him this way and that checking him from top to bottom.

"Time for introductions." She extended her hand toward my dog, a very suspicious Mike. His body language said *I don't know about this. That thing looks dangerous.* With tail stiffly pointed straight back and ears slightly askew, he approached with extreme caution; his neck was stretched forward, front legs angled to the rear, back legs as far back as possible, his whole body extended so far that it looked painful.

"Sniff."

The fur-ball moved.

Now—we had hardwood floors in the house. All were maple, except the bathroom, kitchen, and front porch. My mother loved braided rugs. Braided rugs tend to slide when sideways pressure is applied, and the smaller the rug, the more polished the floor, the greater the slide. My mom's love for her hardwood floors ensured they were well polished.

With coon movement, a retreat was the order of the day for Mike. His neck sucked backward like a turtle's at the same time that his body compacted for flight. His total weight was shifting to the rear, and his legs scrambled to move his body to safety.

Mike applied sideways pressure to one of the smaller rugs in the house. His legs, churning to put distance between him and the baby raccoon, flipped the rug against the wall. SMACK—his chin hit the floor, followed by his left shoulder, twisting his rear legs until they pointed at right angles to the rest of his body.

"YIP!"

I'll have to hand it to him, his legs never stopped pumping, and during the process of righting himself, he ran smack into the wall, glanced off, and disappeared into the kitchen.

"Mike-eee. Here Mike. It's okay, boy. Come-ere. Come on. It's okay. Come on."

Mike peeked around the doorway with a sheepish look, and his tail began to wag as he approached, strangely with less caution than before.

As bold as you please, he marched right up to the killer and smelled, nuzzled, smelled some more, and then licked.

The bond was made.

* * *

Mom was one of those "logical thinkers," especially when it came to feeding wild animals.

On occasions when I brought a baby bird home, we discovered that by using an eyedropper, we were able to force nutrition right down its throat—not the same with a raccoon.

What does a raccoon eat? What does a raccoon without teeth eat, and how does the mother feed her baby?

Mom's solution for feeding the little guy was brilliant in its simplicity. First, a baby bottle that came with one of my sister's dolls. Add a small piece of fur, a remnant of a collar from one of her coats with a slit for the nipple, and we had instant mother raccoon.

Mom, and my friends, Snoopy and his best friend, Mike

Within a few days, we began feeding him solid food. After soaking bread in warm milk, it became almost liquid itself, with enough body to be held on the end of the finger and placed directly into his mouth. He loved it, and before long, we were adding a raw egg to the mixture.

A pet raccoon was a pretty neat thing to have. As he grew, so did the connection between coon, boy, and dog, with a bond that would prove itself many times over during the time that Snoopy elected to stay with us. Mom convinced me that a wild animal should be allowed the freedom to stay or to leave. "Don't build a cage around it. It is wild. If it prefers to leave, allow it to do so. If you love it, let it go, and you will never be sorry." Never caged, he had the run of the house, the run of the yard, and the run of the neighborhood without restraint.

* * *

The sound carried down the hill and echoed between the banks on both sides of the road. It sounded like gravel being poured on a cookie sheet. In reality, it was the sound of tires locked in a skid, spraying gravel and larger rocks onto the underbody of a fast-moving car.

I was sitting on the front steps putting the finishing touches on my new slingshot. My head snapped in the direction of the skidding tires.

It was a pretty old car, nothing special, and it had been coming up the hill. People usually drove too fast when they passed our house, maybe because we were at the crest, and it was second nature to accelerate up the slope, or perhaps the straightness of the road allowed them to build a head of steam. At any rate, this car was now in emergency stop mode.

The driver had red hair. I remember the hair because it was almost so red it looked like the top of his head was on fire. He was looking at our front yard.

"Hey, kid. There's a raccoon! Right there. You better call your dog. The coon may have rabies. Get the dog!"

"Don't worry, mister; he's tame."

"Tame? You're kidding."

"No, sir." I walked toward Snoopy, bent over, and picked him up. He nuzzled my neck, and Mike raised his head to cast a lazy gaze over his shoulder at us.

"I'll be dipped! Where'd you get em?"

"Raised him from a baby. Him and the dog are friends."

He repeated, "I'll be dipped," and pulled his car to the crest. Then, with the engine still running, he hopped out and came toward us.

That's when I learned Snoopy wasn't exactly tame like a cat, and that Mike considered him private property, our exclusive private property.

The instant the guy's foot hit the front yard, Snoopy, who'd been watching him all the way, jumped out of my arms and raced to the base of the closest tree.

Mike didn't move a muscle.

The moment was electric. The air was perfectly still, the summer heat oppressive. The sun, directly overhead, caused beads of sweat to form on the bridge of my nose, and I felt the grass between my toes. The old car sat on the road, engine running. Fire Head's footsteps echoed off each blade of grass, amplified by the moment, and I saw Snoopy at the base of the tree, mouth slightly open, taking deep breaths, his sides heaving, sitting on his haunches while front paws contacted the tree at shoulder level.

It began, like the distant sound of a motorcycle with a bad muffler, or the barely discernible sound of a distant airplane, very softly, but loud enough to disrupt the silence.

Fire Head must have heard the same thing, because he stopped in mid-stride, cocked his head, and strained to locate the source. Softly, but undeniably there, the sound came in waves, long intervals broken by moments of silence, only to be repeated.

I glanced at Mike and could see his upper lip quivering. Mike was growling.

Everything seemed to happen at once.

Fire Head took another step toward Snoopy's tree. Snoopy's survival instincts sprang to life, and Mike's protective juices overflowed. Pieces of bark flew off the tree as the coon clawed frantically to climb out of harm's way, and with a speed that seemed supernatural, Mike was up and at the base hair on end from the top of his head to the tip of his tail, top lip rolled back to expose fangs, and a menacing growl was coming from deep within his body.

Fire Head stopped. "Can you call your dog?" more of a plea than a question.

"Mike…HERE…MIKE."

Mike would do anything for me, and he always came when called… until now.

The dog was unmoving, the coon was securely planted in the crotch of the tree, and Fire Head was like a statue as I moved toward the dog. Taking him by the collar eased the tension in Mike's body, and he turned to me with his sheepish look, as if to say "OOPS.'"

"Sorry, I guess they don't want you to come close."

"Oh, well," he was retreating towards his parked car, "neat." He opened the door, slipped inside, put it in gear, and drove away.

That was it. I knew Snoopy was safe, I knew Fire Head wouldn't try to kidnap him, and I had to believe that all of Fire Head's friends would hear the story, ensuring that at least they would not try to pick up a pet raccoon on Island Park.

* * *

That was the first car that stopped to see the wild raccoon found in our front yard. There were many, many more cars to stop, and many, many more cars that drove by to catch a glimpse of the strange alliance of coon and dog. It was as though the animals knew they were the objects of attention, seeming to perform when a car stopped, or a pedestrian stood and watched.

The routine had Mike lying on his side, motionless, appearing to be out cold. Snoopy started from several feet away, hunching his back—up on all twenty toes—taking baby steps toward the reclining dog. His body was angled to his line of approach, making him appear to float sideways over the lawn, while his best impression of anger was evident by the hiss that came from his open mouth. When he was about a foot away, he charged the reclining dog, pounced on Mike's midsection, and the tussle would begin.

They were the best of friends.

They did have enemies though, enemies in the form of black shadows with teeth; enemies that outweighed Snoopy by 40 pounds and Mike by 20. Their names were Blackie and Muster.

Blackie and Muster were Black Labrador Retrievers. Generally, pretty nice dogs, but not very friendly when they encountered Mike and Snoopy.

There was a thing between Mike and Blackie.

Blackie lived at the bottom of the hill, with a family that recently moved into the neighborhood.

His owners came to the island from the country. I think they were from a farming community in southern Minnesota. Their house was built in a fashion that was typical during that period.

When building in the northern climes, it was advisable to make a structure with a basement. A basement allowed the main floor to hold a reasonably even temperature without fear of having frost and the cold from the frozen ground slowly creeping in from the outside walls. A basement also allowed construction to be completed in two phases. The first phase excavated the basement, and the ceiling was constructed as a flat roof that protected the walled understructure from the outside elements, providing a space for the builder to live while finishing the house. This was known as a basement house, and the island had many.

The owners were like most of the island's early residents—hard-working, diligent, and honest. They built a small chicken coop at the rear of their house and took advantage of the eggs and the occasional chicken dinner it provided.

Blackie was not a smart dog, but he was their pet, entitling him to maintain his space around their house as though it was his kingdom. Mike respected that space and was careful not to intrude.

On the other hand, Mike's kingdom was somewhat more extensive, and he guarded it jealously. He did push the limits of good taste by also considering the road in front of our house as his property.

Morning after morning, the husband climbed into his car and drove up the hill, past our house, down through the saddle, and over the next hill, finally taking a left on the perimeter road, and heading for the bridge that would take him off the island.

Morning after morning, Blackie chased the car up the hill.

Morning after morning, Mike challenged him in front of the house, and they had a short but vicious fight, after which Blackie retreated to the bottom of the hill, and his own personal kingdom.

It got to the point that when Mike ran to challenge Blackie, the poor Labrador just sat down right in the middle of the road. Mike circled, every hair on his back straight up, while Blackie just sat there, staring straight ahead. Mike, lip peeled back to show formidable fangs, growled, sniffed, turned his back, and scratched loose gravel towards the immobile Lab. He tried everything to get a reaction. Nothing! This must have been a major source of frustration, but he eventually turned and walked stiff-legged, back to the yard.

One day, something happened that stopped car-chasing altogether.

The car passed, Blackie followed. Mike intercepted. Blackie plopped down in the middle of the road. Mike did his best to start a fight. Blackie sat there, unmoving. Mike circled a few times as I tried to call him back into the yard, and horror of horrors, without warning, proceeded to lift his leg and void his bladder on the poor Labrador's back. Head high, he pranced back to the front yard while Blackie got to his feet and headed for home. That was the last time Blackie followed up the hill.

* * *

One afternoon, I was sitting on the porch reading a comic book. As usual, the day was hot and still. Mike was at the other end of the porch, lying in the shade on the bare linoleum, and Snoopy was outside someplace doing his own thing.

Suddenly there was a scream.

Mike beat me to the screen door.

BLAM! He hit it with his head, and it flew open against the spring. Before it could recoil back to the closed position, he was off the front steps, and halfway to the driveway, with me in hot pursuit. He streaked across the driveway and down the steep slope on the other side, heading in the direction of the scream.

Again, the terrible scream. This time I saw the source.

Snoopy was desperately trying to evade the jaws of one of the black labs, while the other was charging along the hill, intent on having raccoon for lunch. From the opposite direction, racing at top speed, was Snoopy's friend, Mike.

It was evident that Mike and the lab would reach Snoopy at about the same time. What was not so evident was the result of that meeting.

It was like a scene from a Saturday movie. Only it was happening right before my eyes. Even today, it replays as in slow motion.

Snoopy stood, hunched, with his back arched, and his tail pointed straight up, every hair on his body electrified, trying to look bigger and more formidable than he really was. His eyes were fixed on Muster, who stood motionless, slather dripping from an open mouth.

Blackie was charging at full speed directly down the hill toward Snoopy; his eyes fixed on the fur-ball that would soon be his prize, total concentration on the raccoon just feet ahead.

On the other side, Mike The Athlete, racing to protect his friend, eyes fixed on the charging Blackie, total concentration on stopping the black shadow, before he could reach his goal.

Bound by bound, Blackie closed the distance. Forty feet—eyes intent, fixed on the target—Thirty feet, saliva streaming from the corners of his mouth—Twenty feet, silent running, two more bounds and that fur-ball is history—Ten feet, teeth bared, fangs clicking on the bottom teeth as the mouth silently opened and closed—POUNCE, sweet victory is mine!

He never knew what hit him.

Blackie was caught broadside, fully extended, and I could hear the breath leave his lungs as he was hit in midair. He didn't have a chance.

Mike, all forty pounds of him, left the ground, and was gaining momentum when they collided. His target, the sixty-pound black shadow, was descending toward his prey, momentum spent, jaws about to close on his lunch. No contest.

"YIP!" was all the poor lab could say as he hit the ground, chin scraping the grass for the entire ten feet it took before he twisted into a ball, and rolled head over heels, coming to rest at the feet of his evil partner Muster.

A look of dismay was written on his face as he picked himself up. Muster looked at him, head cocked to one side, equal dismay in his eyes trying to figure out what had just happened.

Blackie shook his head and regained what was left of his composure. Together they turned as one to face in the direction of their one-time lunch.

What was this?

Just a moment ago, they were inches away from their prize. Surrounded and alone, there was no escape for the enemy raccoon, when all of a sudden, there was a new game, and one that gave them a reason to pause.

There stood their lunch, back arched, lips rolled back, a menacing and very serious growl coming from his 20-pound body. Straddling this bundle of explosive fury was the spoiler known as Mike.

The top of Snoopy's arched back was in contact with Mike's heaving chest as he stood between his forelegs. Together they stood, teeth bared, eyes blazing, ready to do battle, daring Muster and Blackie to come within range.

I raced towards the scene of the standoff, scared to death, and bursting with pride at the same time.

"HEY! GET OUTTA HERE!"

In retrospect, I think the lab duo welcomed the distraction, because they immediately turned, tucked their tails between their legs and beat it towards Blackie's kingdom.

I stopped, afraid to approach the very scary and serious countenance presented by the dog-coon combination.

"Mike!" his head turned.

"Snoopy, here, boy." His snarl stopped, and he looked up at his protector. Mike sniffed and nuzzled, Snoopy sniffed and nuzzled, his tongue touching Mike's chin, and they both walked to where I stood. I swear I could see the pride in their faces.

I sat on the grass, and the three of us wrestled and played while I checked every inch of Snoopy's body for damage, finding none.

I'm sure that they, as much as I, knew how lucky we had been. It was the only time that Snoopy was caught in the open, although he continued to roam freely and enjoyed having the run of the house, coming and going as he wished. In retrospect, I don't recall a single time that Snoopy had a potty accident inside.

* * *

It was the comings and goings that were really quite impressive, and a testament to the intelligence behind his black eyes. Snoopy learned to open the screen door leading into the porch, and with that skill, gained independence beyond rational expectations.

It was no big deal for him to press against the door with his front paws while on the inside, quietly slipping through the opening before the spring slapped it closed again. It was something entirely different for him to learn to open the door from the outside.

He learned that if he put one of his shoulders on the flagstone, he could place his claws in the crack between the threshold and the bottom of the door. A simple pulling action caused the door to swing outward, and he simply got to his feet, pushed the door farther open with his other front leg, and entered the porch.

I don't know if all raccoons are as smart as Snoopy or whether he was exceptional, but he learned things, and once learned, he never forgot them.

It wasn't long before he was coming in the basement door.

The door had a handle and thumb latch mechanism that required pulling on the handle as the thumb latch was depressed. Snoopy reached up, grabbed the bottom of the handle, and pulled himself up to the point that allowed him to place his other front paw on the latch, and pulling it down, pushed on the doorframe with his rear leg. Quite unbelievable.

The two of us played for hours. One of his favorite games took place on the porch and required the smooth surface of the linoleum covering the entire floor.

He pestered me, regardless of where I was in the house until I followed him to the porch. Once there, he attacked me in apparent anger, and I pushed him away. Rolling him onto his back, I spun him round and round as his feet clawed the air, and his mouth harmlessly opened and closed on my wrists. I sent him sliding along the linoleum towards the other end of the porch, his body twisting, and turning trying to get himself upright during his slide.

As soon as he righted himself, he came towards me with a menacing growl and hunched back. With his sideways saunter, he charged straight ahead into my waiting hands, where he was flipped on his back, twirled, and sent on his slide again. He loved the game and kept it going until I called it quits.

Raccoons can grasp items between both front paws, and manipulate them like they had hands. Snoopy dipped his food in the water dish before putting it in his mouth, resulting in some comical moments when he tried to eat fresh bread or other baked goods. A piece went into the water as a solid, but after being rolled and turned while submerged, it turned to mush before he could get it into his mouth.

I believe the real reason he washed his food was that he had little or no saliva. He merely needed the moisture to help him swallow. This apparent fact was driven home one day when I fed him a caramel. The poor guy would have choked had I not been there to remove the barely moist mass from his throat.

He also loved to reach into the toes of Dad's shoes to retrieve things we dropped there. His favorite was one or two marbles from my marble pouch. He sat on his haunches, the heel of the shoe pulled into his belly, and fished into the toe with his front legs up to the elbow, all the while looking around the room as he rolled the marble between his front paws. Once he had a firm grip, he extracted his prize, only to examine and release it, at which point it would roll back into the toe. The process was repeated time and again.

Snoopy also came when called.

Most times, he stayed pretty close to the house, but there was no doubt that the response was his idea. He ran directly to me and waited for me to pick him up. I buried my face in his belly as he excitedly mauled my head with his paws.

As he got older, it was not unusual for him to disappear for days at a time.

I remember our family having company at the house; company that wanted to see the raccoon we had as a pet. I was willing to make a try at calling him, so I went out the basement door, stepped behind the house facing the swamp, and began calling his name. I called for about five minutes before going back inside to tell the company they were out of luck. Snoopy was nowhere in sight.

As my parents visited in the living room with their guests, we heard a kitchen drawer being pulled out. I peeked around the kitchen entrance, and there he was, climbing up the front of the drawers.

Sure enough, he had let himself in the basement door, come up the steps, and gone directly to the drawer he knew my mother stocked with hard, stale bread. It was "his drawer."

As was his custom, he opened it, removed a dried roll, and holding it in his mouth, climbed the drawer pulls unto the counter, where he sat and enjoyed his meal by the sink.

Needless to say, the houseguests were pleased with the encounter.

As great as that visit was, it was his last trip home that stands out in my memory.

We hadn't seen him for several weeks, and as I lay in bed, I remember wondering if I'd ever see him again.

"Dale, will you come out here, please. Now!"

The urgency in her voice made me climb quickly out of bed, and head for the other room where she met me with an ashen face.

"Go look in the kitchen. But be careful! He's really big."

As I turned the corner into the dining room, I looked through the archway leading to the kitchen. I approached with caution, not knowing what to expect. When I reached the opening, I saw what startled my mother out of about five years of her life.

On the counter next to the sink, sat the largest raccoon I ever saw; his furry coat filled the opening between the countertop and the bottom of the cupboard, and his bushy ring-tail, curled around his body as he looked in my direction, a dry biscuit between his front paws. His eyes were wide, and I knew immediately he wasn't a danger. I approached, repeating his name.

"Snoopy, hi boy—Snoopy, how are ya—Snoopy's got bread." He just looked at me.

He stopped twisting the biscuit between his paws and stared in my direction as I approached. I held my hands at my sides, offering him the top of my head, laying my cheek on the counter. He immediately began to nuzzle my ear, and I knew all was well.

I picked him up and shoved my face into his furry belly as he stroked the back of my head with his front paws. We continued to nuzzle each other while I walked into the living room.

It was special, as he laid on his back in my arms stroking my neck and cheeks, and all too soon, he squirmed in my arms, fell to the floor landing on all fours, and moved toward the screen door.

In a flash, he was gone. I marveled at the visit, even then. It was as though he came back on a very special night to say a very special good-bye. I went to bed that night and slept the sleep of contentment. It was the last time he came into the house.

One night the following spring, Mike, who was in the basement, awakened me with his barking. I peeked out the back bedroom door, and there, in a mid-sized maple growing about ten feet from the rear of the back porch, was an adult raccoon. It looked at me, unafraid as I gazed into its open face.

There was a movement to my right. Turning, I saw four baby bandits, eyes masked, and tails ringed, climbing and playing on a trailer my father parked behind the house. I looked back at the tree, and the raccoon was gone.

I had been given a wonderful gift. Snoopy brought his family to meet me.

I love him as much today as I did when we were partners, with Mike, on the island.

CHAPTER 21

Graduating to the Working World

When I was fourteen, I knew I had to make my own money. One of the neighbors was a partner in a water drilling company, and his son, Jerry, was a friend of mine. We worked for his dad for a single day collecting a small paycheck; nevertheless, my first pay for work performed.

My second attempt was to try my hand at caddying. The closest golf course to Island Park was the Lafayette Club, situated on the south side of Crystal Bay, Lake Minnetonka. It was a beautiful piece of property that stretched from Crystal Bay to County Road Fifteen, running between Wayzata and Navarre. That stretch of road passed some of the most expensive properties around the lake, following the shoreline around Browns Bay, Smiths Bay, and finally, Lafayette Bay.

I caddied at Lafayette about seven hours before deciding it wasn't my cup of tea. I worked a single loop, carrying for a middle-aged woman who was a terrible golfer. Her tongue was as sharp as a samurai blade, and she had the personality of a cornered rat. I got five dollars plus a fifty-cent tip for eighteen holes. I never went back.

A week or so later, I hitchhiked closer to Wayzata and tried the Woodhill Country Club. I followed the access road from county road

15, which wound its way to the clubhouse, and after a little searching and asking questions, I crossed the sixth fairway running between the pro shop and the caddy shack and got my first real taste of life as a caddy.

Unlike Lafayette, where every head turned to examine the new guy, I walked into the caddy-yard unnoticed. Kids were shooting baskets on the improvised court, while others were playing cards or sitting around trading lies.

The pro shop must have called the caddy master to announce my coming because he was waiting at the door of the shack to welcome me aboard. He stood about five-foot-six, two-inch cigar stub firmly in place on the left side of his mouth, itself situated in a round head devoid of hair. He had a light reddish complexion with a bulbous nose reminiscent of W.C. Fields, and his first priority was to sell me a hot dog.

"What's your name, boy?" The cigar bounced.

"Dale."

"Ya got a last name?"

"Swanson."

"I'm Herb. I'm caddy master, and I decide who gets the loops. I sell hot dogs, pop, and candy. You buy my stuff, and I'll take care o'ya. Ain't no fightin' or teasin' or your gone. Don't want no cussin' either."

That was my introduction to Woodhill Country Club and the grumpy, but fair, Herb Finney.

I soon learned his habit of using only the last names of his caddies. We'd hear the phone ring; he'd pick it up, scribble something on a notepad, step to the door, and call out someone's name. The cigar butt was omnipresent but never lit.

"Niedermeyer, this one's for you."

Niedermeyer, McDonald, Mittlestaedt, Simar, or whoever was called, moved with haste to pick the scorecard from his hand, head across the sixth fairway to pick up the golfers' clubs from the pro shop and meet them at the first tee.

It didn't take Herb long to recognize my ineptitude as a caddy, so he sent me with experienced caddies to learn the ropes. Many times, when there was a threesome, he called my name, and I carried a single bag while the other kid carried doubles. After about two weeks, I was allowed to carry for two ladies who played only nine holes. Eventually, I became proficient enough for Herb to send me with the occasional senior club member.

Woodhill Country Club was "old money." Names recognized by nearly all Minnesotans. Scott, Whitney, Pillsbury, Heffelfinger, and a host of others made up the membership, and at one time or another, I caddied for most of them. In fact, John S. Pillsbury Sr. was responsible for Herb promoting me to "A" caddy. According to Herb, Mr. Pillsbury gave me a good review, and this was my reward, entitling me to move from twelve to eighteen dollars for 18-hole doubles. In addition to the actual pay, there was usually a significant tip when the golfer had a good round. It was our job to ensure no lost balls, eagerly climbing into dense bushes, briars, and poison ivy to find errant shots. We got to know the capabilities of each golfer and advised distance and club selection when asked.

I made pretty good money and stashed it under Dad's fireman's uniform hat in the hall closet. I had a roll of bills secured by a rubber band, and it just got bigger and bigger.

By this time, Dad had a job with the local school district as a custodian. He realized that to earn advancement, he needed a first-class boiler-engineering license. He and Mom were floundering just trying to make ends meet, and I had this stash of rolled bills in the hall closet. Dad enrolled at Dunwoody Institute, got his license, and the promotion he deserved.

After my second summer at Woodhill, I got an after-school and weekend job at Spring Park Hardware. Located in Skunk Hollow, across the street from the Downbeat and Lakeview bars, it was a vintage hardware store in an old building, the kind of place that could yield treasures down every aisle. Ray Jarvey and Harley Towner were partners, and the store had darn near anything you could think of, and a few things that had attained obsolescence years earlier.

Our proximity to the bars across the road led to one specific episode that haunts me yet today, for reasons, which will become evident.

It was a Saturday evening. Dusk had settled in, and darkness was just around the corner, the doors locked for the night. Harley was in the office, and I was straightening a few items when there was tapping on the front door. I walked to the inside of the door and found an intoxicated man on the other side, demanding entry. Seems when he left the house that morning, he was supposed to arrange to have us deliver a large tank of propane. Finding himself drunk as a skunk at days end, he finally realized he had not yet ordered the propane, and needed to get it done before he went home. He refused to leave, so Harley came to handle the situation. The guy mumbled his predicament, and Harley, compassionate man that he was, refused delivery but agreed to have me load the tank in the guy's car. I moved to the platform out back while he drove his car around.

As I maneuvered the tank toward the edge of the platform, he asked a question.

"Ya got a toilet back here?"

"No, sir. No toilet."

"Ya sure? Man, I gotta find a toilet."

"No, sir. No toilet."

"Uuuhhh, boy, that's not good."

"Where should I put the tank, sir?"

"Put er in the front sheet."

"I don't know if it'll fit."

"Wedge er in."

As I worked to get the one hundred plus pound tank into the passenger seat, the guy leaned against the side of the car, grimaced, and commenced to have diarrhea in his pants. Like it happened every day, he casually walked around the front of the car, leaving a trail in his wake, opened the driver's door, slid behind the wheel, and headed for home. I've always wondered how the remainder of his evening went.

Through my connection with Spring Park hardware, the following summer, I began mowing the lawns for two neighbors who lived on Crystal Bay, just beyond Coffee Bridge.

Charlie Bush and Earl King were like a good scotch and soda. Charlie bought a reel mower—Earl purchased a reel mower, both self-propelled. Charlie had specifics on how he wanted his lawn cut and trimmed—Earl adopted the same requirements, usually with a new wrinkle or two, just to let me know he was his own man.

It was the perfect arrangement for me. On Tuesdays, I would caddy till early afternoon, then head for the lawn jobs. When there was extra work associated with the mowing, there was flexibility in my schedule to accommodate it.

There were other jobs as well, including doing some work for Bill Netka. His furniture store was in the old Mound Theatre, and Bill wanted the floor leveled into terraced segments for staging his furniture. I was hired, along with Mike Mittlestaedt, my good friend and caddy partner at Woodhill. It was the summer before my senior year in high school and was a pretty miserable job. With typical summer temperatures and high humidity, we were hauling, leveling, and packing sand with shovels, wheelbarrows, and hand tampers. I remember it, of all my odd jobs while in high school, as the one I liked the least.

Mike and I determined we would enlist in the armed forces after graduation, and my family started to make inquiries around those plans. The recruiters came to the house, and I was given a few tests to determine my potential. It turned out the Navy offered the best possibilities for meaningful training, so that was the unanimous selection.

As the last adventure, the summer after graduation, Mike and I planned to hitchhike to his grandfather's house in Milbank, South Dakota. I'm not sure how we sold our parents on the idea, but the trip came to fruition, and we left home on a Saturday morning with a bag lunch and a pocketful of expectations. I remember only parts of the trip, but somewhere along the way, we dawdled in a field where I found an old shotgun. Rusted and inoperable, we nonetheless toted the thing home. Times were different then. I can't imagine anyone picking up a couple of teenagers with a shotgun under their arm, but we hitched our way home without incident, and the old gun now resides in my house, rust intact, a reminder of simpler times.

END

Next—Into the U.S. Navy and beyond

CPSIA information can be obtained
at www.ICGtesting.com
Printed in the USA
BVHW080058050220
571463BV00003B/8

9 780986 326769